Barndominiums

Quarto.com

© 2023 Quarto Publishing Group USA Inc.

First Published in 2023 by Cool Springs Press, an imprint of The Quarto Group,
100 Cummings Center, Suite 265-D, Beverly, MA 01915, USA.
T (978) 282-9590 F (978) 283-2742

Cool Springs Press titles are also available at discount for retail, wholesale, promotional, and bulk purchase. For details, contact the Special Sales Manager by email at specialsales@quarto.com or by mail at The Quarto Group, Attn: Special Sales Manager, 100 Cummings Center, Suite 265-D, Beverly, MA 01915, USA.

27 26 25 24   2 3 4 5

ISBN: 978-0-7603-8226-4

Digital edition published in 2023
eISBN: 978-0-7603-8227-1

Library of Congress Cataloging-in-Publication Data available

Design and Page Layout: Megan Jones Design
Cover Image: Cody Wortmann | Courtesy Timberlyne. Timberlyne enriches lives with timber structures that harness the beauty, sustainability, and strength of wood. www.timberlyne.com
Illustration: Christopher Mills Illustration on pages 80, 98, 118, 119, 121, and 172

Printed in China

Barndominiums

YOUR GUIDE TO A PERFECT, INEXPENSIVE DREAM HOME

CHRIS PETERSON

COOL
SPRINGS
PRESS

Contents

Introduction:
A New Frontier in Housing

You may never have heard of a barndominium. You're not alone. A lot of people have no clue what it is exactly, but it's a term well worth learning. That funny word could be your affordable path to a wonderful new home in a real estate market that seems increasingly untethered from economic reality.

A mashup of "barn" and "condominium," the term means a home created inside a traditional barn structure. Barndominiums, "barndos" for short, are often built of prefab steel components. They can also be custom steel structures or built with timbers or even conventional wood frames. A barndo is normally built on a concrete slab. Far less commonly, they are built on stem-wall foundations, and very rarely, on full basements.

The barndo's defining characteristic is a roof entirely supported by exterior walls. This creates almost unlimited options in floor-plan design by eliminating interior, load-bearing walls.

Barndos are incredibly durable, versatile, economical, and even environmentally friendly. They look like other homes inside. But make no mistake—a barndominium is completely different. That's because a barndominium is more than just a building or a home. Living in a barndominium is a wonderful, fulfilling way of life.

THE OLD NEW IDEA

Believe it or not, the barndominium concept dates to 1989, when a Connecticut realtor invented the word. He hoped to sell horse-country folks on the idea of combining a home and a stable into one compelling structure. He saw dollar signs in matching local horse lovers and the many derelict barns in the region.

The idea did not catch on. Well, at least not until 2016. That's when Chip and Joanna Gaines brought the word and the concept back to life in an episode of their hit HGTV show, *Fixer Upper*. They dedicated the episode to a gorgeous renovation of a barn, revealing the interior-design magic concealed in these simple rectangular structures. Millions of viewers got a firsthand look at what a barndominium was and could be.

The simplest and least expensive barndominiums follow the basic rectangular design of most working barns. This one includes a covered patio with an unrivaled view, standalone solar panels to reduce energy costs, and a color meant to blend seamlessly into the surroundings.

A NEW TREND FOCUSED ON "NEW"

Even though that high-profile barn conversion inspired what became a nationwide trend, most barndominiums are built new. Precious few barns are available for conversion, and existing structures are in such rough condition that converting them can be just as expensive as building new. Starting from scratch means you can plan exactly what you want, where you want it. That is why this book focuses on new construction, although much of the information applies equally well to renovations of existing barns.

No matter how you create yours, it's about much more than four tall walls and a big end door. A barndominium is as much idea as structure; it's about getting back to the heart of the Old West romantic ideal of room to be just who you are, a slow pace, a life well lived, and timeless country style.

Barndominium allure started in a handful of Bible Belt states: Georgia, Alabama, Oklahoma, and, most popularly, Texas. It was only natural that the trend would first find footing where people could buy large, rural property lots cheaply. Barndominiums go hand in hand with ample acreage.

The popularity has only grown. You can now find barndominium manufacturers, suppliers, builders, and devotees in most western and southern states, and even in the Midwest.

The appeal is the same no matter where you build. The construction method creates a wide-open interior, physically and conceptually. You can vary the exterior as well. You might include a simple wraparound patio, or a full-blown outdoor kitchen as a seamless extension of the interior space. The building provides an easily adaptable canvas for your imagination.

Although you can buy smaller models, barndominiums commonly measure 3,000 square feet (280 square m) or larger. That represents a mother lode of open square footage and design potential for anyone willing to look beyond a conventional house.

As this eye-catching home illustrates, a modest, affordable steel barndo needn't look mundane. This home is a pole-barn model and includes distinctive twin dormers that increase natural light.

Build a two-story interior or create a single-level layout with a loft and soaring vaulted ceilings. Bring a jaw-dropping open floor plan to life or incorporate a more traditional room-by-room layout.

Because they are based on working buildings that house farm animals and equipment and even businesses, barndominiums naturally lend themselves to a combination of functions. Many owners set aside one end or even one-half of the structure for a hobby area, a workshop, a man (or woman) cave, or just a garage. You can even build in stables and share your living space with a few equine friends, if your local zoning allows.

A barndominium is never *just* a place to lay your head or keep your stuff; it's a haven where you can live well, work hard, play harder, and enjoy every moment.

WHY A BARNDO?

The American dream of buying a new home has become a nightmare. Real estate markets across the country have gone more than a little bit crazy. Home prices have skyrocketed since bottoming out during the sub-prime mortgage crisis of 2008. Historically low mortgage interest rates and a persistently strong economy threw fire on an overheated real estate market.

Even accounting for inflation, national average home prices have increased as much as 10 percent per year, each of the last five years. In some major metropolitan areas, that increase is closer to 15 percent per year. Those figures are far above the average worker's increase in wages over the same period.

Sadly, those realities have put home buying out of the reach of many. Building a new home is hardly a better option. It's not only expensive, but the most desirable cities and towns are running out of buildable lots.

So, what are prospective home buyers to do? Find cheaper property in an outlying area, build a barndominium, and create their own little slice of heaven, that's what.

If you buy a prefab steel package, the price will rise and fall more quickly and drastically than the price of wood. Once you've decided on a barndo, lock in the price and get it in writing.

The (Potentially) Low-Cost Option

The cost of building a new home varies widely across the nation but averages around $130 to $145 per square foot (.30 m) for a traditional 2,000-square-foot (610-square m) , wood-frame structure.

Barndominium costs? They average $70 to $120 per square foot (per .30 m) in the United States (to prep the site, construct, plumb, wire, and insulate the shell). That leaves a lot left over to buy interior finishes, appliances, and surfaces.

Consider one of the hottest barndo states—Texas. The cost of the average new home there is about $130 per square foot (.30 m). Buy a steel barndominium prefab "kit" from one of the several Texas-based manufacturers, and you're looking at spending between $45 to $65 per square foot (.30 m) for a fully assembled and insulated shell, with windows and doors. That leaves you somewhere between $75,000 and $130,000 to splurge on a dream interior. Be just slightly frugal in your build choices and the final cost will be significantly less than that of the average traditional new home. The payoff is a custom home designed to suit your tastes, with far more space than the average American residence.

New barndominiums can offer far more energy efficiency than the average residential structure. Depending on the type of interior framing, a barndominium may be able to accommodate wall and ceiling insulation almost twice as deep as in a stick-frame house, offering significantly higher R-value. Many barndo owners also opt for a special reflective roof coating, further reducing energy costs by as much as 30 percent.

Here's a rough breakdown of the budget to build one of these unique structures, not counting the cost of the land. Always account for building permits and processing fees; those range from $400 to $2,000, depending on the state and locality.

Barndominium Balance Sheet

The costs here are compiled from a review of estimates across the United States, including from local municipalities. Local costs will vary.

Engineered slab	$6.20 per square foot (0.3 m). 6" (15 cm) depth. Additional depth and reinforcement if required by local code may increase cost.
Shell assembly	$100 per square foot (0.3 m) includes prefab steel kit, construction, plumbing, wiring, and insulation. * The DIY option would reduce construction costs by 30–40%.
Delivery	10% of kit cost. This may be negotiable, depending on how far the home site is from the manufacturer'sfacility.
Interior finishing	$25–$100 psf (0.3 m) This wide range reflects the extensive options among available finishes, features, and fixtures, including interior framing possibilities (e.g., a single-level open floor plan will need far less framing than a two-story, multi-room layout).

POTENTIAL ADDITIONAL COSTS

Paved road to home	$55–$85 per linear foot (0.3 m)
Gravel road to home	$20 per linear foot (0.3 m)
Well	$25–$65 per foot (0.3 m) of depth (varies based on soil condition, well diameter, access to site, and other factors. National average for residential wells is $3,750–$15,300).
Septic system	$6,000–$20,000 (includes complete setup, and varies based on number of household users, site preparation, etc.)
Run new power	$100 per linear foot (0.3 m). Varies widely depending on existing line services, route from power source to home site, and other variables.

THE GREEN HOME

A great number of barndominiums built today are steel shells with traditional stick framing inside (lumber studs, joists, and headers). Metal or steel prefab panels don't involve the carbon release that cutting and processing lumber does. Prefab steel components and panels are also manufactured to exact specifications, eliminating waste. Compare that to the average 10 percent waste in cutting wood members for a stick-frame home, and you'll see the environmental advantage. Many manufacturers even use recycled steel for as much as 90 percent of their products. In short, a steel barndo often saves energy and materials in production and sends far less construction waste to a landfill.

But some barndos are hybrids, with partial steel frames and one or more exterior walls framed in wood. Timber-frame structures, using oversized posts, beams, and trusses, are also popular because of wood's (much pricier) unique beauty, warmth, and distinctive character.

The integrity of the blown-in foam insulation used to insulate most modern barndominiums means that the home uses much less energy for heating and cooling. South-facing barndo roofs are excellent sites for a bank of solar panels.

DESIGN FLEXIBILITY

Anyone who is enchanted by a barn's evocative, rustic nature and simple appearance will find barndos' distinctive design alluring. The essence of the wide-open West, of an America full of potential, is captured in the barn's traditional shape and appearance. It's no accident that barndominiums are often situated on larger rural property lots. Barndos offer a slower, "country" lifestyle, with privacy and spacious outdoor areas.

Many find the barndominium's biggest selling point is the raw potential inside its exceptionally large empty interior spaces. The raw square footage is a most inviting canvas. Because the exterior walls support the entire structure, barndominiums have no interior load-bearing walls. Put walls where you want them.

One caveat, though: Because they support the whole structure, steel posts and trusses must be placed at certain points. That will dictate window and door placement, which may affect your interior design. The design potential is still greater than with a traditional stick-built house.

Can you dream the home fantastic? If so, you can probably realize that vision inside your new barndominium shell. Fashion a unique floor plan perfectly customized to your family's needs. Never lack for storage again. Display oversized art and pictures exactly how you want to. The hardest part? Sifting through all those options.

Solar panels fit beautifully on barndominium roofs. The panels offer some energy independence, drastically lowering energy costs, and helping the environment. Many states offer rebates on solar panel installation cost.

Barndos lend themselves to using rough-and-ready natural materials, like the exposed brick, quarter-sawn wood plank flooring, and other materials inside this home.

Barndos' large space and distinctive architectural style naturally lend themselves to eye-catching design features. These include, among many others:

- Vaulted ceilings and large window walls

- Spiral or custom-designed staircases

- Interior sliding barn doors

- Movable partition walls

- Showcase fireplaces and/or firepits

- Natural wood and stone surfaces

- Cupolas and weathervanes

Because barndos naturally have barn doors to maintain the integrity of the look, your home can easily accommodate a storage and work area for vehicles of all shapes and sizes. Ceilings that average 14 feet (4.3 m) high mean even full-size RVs will fit. Want to customize that motorcycle? How about a fully outfitted workshop right through your kitchen door? Like to keep your boat and ATV out of the elements when not in use? Never fear: there is plenty of space for all your toys.

SAFETY AND DURABILITY

Build a home from a steel frame and metal siding and you've constructed a safe, resilient structure. The typical barndominium shell is fire-resistant, termite-proof, and provides an inhospitable surface for mold and mildew. Although most owners choose to use wood framing inside the barndominium, the outer shell's integrity is exceptional.

A timber-framed or wood-pole barn barndominium involves a conscious swap: more charming appearance and the warmth of wood, with more susceptibility to the elements and insects. However, both options feature incredibly durable construction that offers exceptional longevity and resistance to wind loads.

Steel barndominiums also need less maintenance than wood-framed homes. Paint bonds more securely and permanently to a steel panel surface, and metal siding does not crack or fracture like a wood or stucco wall can. Depending on the color, the paint on a barndominium's steel walls is often under warranty for 25 to 40 years.

Wood framed post-and-beam or pole-barn structures are more susceptible to insect damage and other issues, but are also very solid structures that stand up to extreme weather events including tornadoes. Many people also find them aesthetically more pleasing and more amenable for use as a residential structure.

For the most natural look, site a barndominium where you can keep as much existing vegetation as possible. Here, an old-growth tree helps create the impression that the barndo has always been there.

WHAT TYPE OF BARNDO?

The first barndominiums converted existing barns, usually wood-pole barns, into living spaces. A range of steel-building manufacturers quickly recognized the potential. They already produced all-in-one, bolt-up component packages for industrial and commercial steel buildings. So, it wasn't hard for them to shift gears and market steel barndominium "kits" to potential homeowners.

Reality check: if your idea of a "kit" is two pages of instructions and an afternoon of paint-by-number assembly, you might be in for a shock. Prefab bolt-up systems—barndo kits—do include all the components and hardware needed to construct a barndominium shell. But they also come with assembly instructions that can run dozens to a hundred pages. More complex erector set than simple box, these buildings are often manufactured to order.

Many skilled DIY homeowners have built their own post-frame barndominiums, but if you go down that road, it's important to understand what you're attempting and the scope of the work.

Construction requires heavy equipment, such as a scissor lift, familiarity with construction tools like welding rigs, and comfort with precision measurements and fabrication. You also need knowledge of codes and best construction standards and practices, especially if you're assembling a metal building. A timber-frame structure requires a craftsman's skills and only an experienced builder should tackle it.

Either way, most people hire a builder or general contractor who can easily coordinate necessary permits and installation of plumbing, wiring, and HVAC (heating, ventilating and air-conditioning) systems along with the building construction. Even among prefab steel barndominiums, materials, features, and processes vary astoundingly, much more than with traditional stick-built homes.

If you decide to be your own builder, you'll need energy, patience, much more time than the process normally takes, attention to detail, and comfort with learning on the fly. Most people go with a pro. In either case, this book provides a general overview of the different stages of construction, and different choices you'll make along the way.

Many potential barndo owners choose a soup-to-nuts company offering complete services, from initial cost estimating and design, to manufacturing building components, providing construction services, and even offering interior finishing expertise. If you'd prefer to have expert guidance and minimal involvement through the whole process, this type of company is ideal for you.

Here are the basic barndominium types, with the first two known as "post frame" because beefy posts support the building along side walls. None of the five types requires interior load-bearing walls.

» **Steel frame.** This is the most common style, normally built on a concrete slab. Prefab steel panels and columns are manufactured to suit the project, eliminating waste in a low-cost, high-efficiency production process. Components are fabricated quickly and trucked to the job site. Manufacturers supply detailed assembly instructions. Once off-loaded, the shell can be constructed in a week, but usually takes around two weeks, unless it's a DIY build, which takes much longer. The posts can be spaced widely apart while maintaining structural integrity. Steel trusses bridge across side wall posts. Homeowners often paint them if they will be exposed. Steel barndominium components have relatively long warranties, often 30 to 50 years on structural members, and 25 years on exterior panels.

A steel building need not lack flair. As this stunning structure illustrates, red paint with black trim offers a simple and dramatic style.

From the outside, you often can't tell pole barn structures from their steel post-frame cousins. This two-story beauty boasts exceptional space inside for both a work garage and living quarters.

» **Pole barn.** A more traditional form of barn construction, this involves anchoring laminated pressure-treated timbers (or, in some cases, steel poles) 3 to 6 feet (1–2 m) in the ground to support the walls and clear-span roof trusses. Where once the "poles" were left in contact with the soil and prone to moisture damage and decay, now poles are pressure-treated wood protected from soil contact. They can easily last decades, depending on how they are secured in the ground (see page 119 for options). Some manufacturers offer poles bolted to a slab foundation. Embedded poles involve slightly more complex installation, but manufacturers supply the prefab components that make assembly as easy as with steel post-frame barndominiums.

» **Hybrid.** This is an option for those who like the benefits of a steel building but want to customize beyond a rectangle or L shape. Most of the structure is a steel post frame, with one or more walls built of traditional stick framing. Properly engineered support for roof trusses is key to a successful hybrid build.

» **Post and beam.** A middle ground between traditional pole barns and timber-framed structures, post-and-beam barns are built with less complicated joinery than that used in a fully timber-framed structure. As with timber framing, post-and-beam barns are meant to capture the warmth and appeal of wood. Called "hybrids in the industry," some use prefab steel panels with wood beams and posts. That translates to less expense and faster construction.

A post-and-beam barndo extension on an existing house awaits a steel roof and steel wall panels.

A fully timber-framed barndominium showcases craftsmanship and is an engaging and welcoming structure.

» **Timber frame.** Timber-frame barndos cost more than steel ones but are the height of craftsmanship. They have a more authentic "barn" look and feel, with the luxury and warmth of a wood home. Heavy beams crisscross the main space and can support lofts or other structures. They provide an attractive visual and are usually left exposed. Timber posts are much larger than traditional stick-frame studs, usually 8×8 in. (20×20 cm). They are bolted to the foundation and can be spaced far apart. Timber barndominiums are more susceptible to fire and insects but, built correctly, they can last a century. As with steel barndominiums, you can buy timber-frame models as packages. These include precision-cut framing members, structural insulated panel (SIP) exterior wall cladding, hardware, and other necessary components.

CHALLENGES AND REQUIREMENTS

Even small barndominiums are sizable structures. Ideally, you should build on at least an acre (4047 square m), preferably larger. Homeowners priced out of local real estate markets can afford a larger parcel of land in metropolitan or suburban areas. Factors to consider:

- **Codes.** Before you commit to a piece of property, you must investigate local codes. In rare cases, local codes may preclude or restrict building living quarters in barn structures. But if you have bought a rural property lot under county administration versus within an incorporated city, the code burden will be less. In fact, the permitting and approval process will likely be easier, quicker, and less expensive than in an urban or suburban area.

  Due diligence involves talking to a knowledgeable, licensed contractor or a local building inspector. Older local codes may not clearly regulate barndominiums or specify which codes the structure has to comply with. Because local inspectors will approve different stages of construction, you'll want to know how they interpret the codes. Of course, if you're using a full-service contractor for the entire project, that professional will ensure code compliance.

- **Land.** Your building lot may present certain challenges, even before you lay the foundation. First, how close is the property to the nearest paved road? The answer will influence the best site for the barndominium. This is where a seasoned professional, a local surveyor or a contractor, can be a huge help in heading off future problems. Find out how much time, effort, and expense your contractor or sub-contractor needs to put into preparing the job site for construction (e.g., grading, improving drainage, etc.). Estimate how much it will cost to run services to the building and build an access road or driveway. Although a compacted dirt road (known in the industry as "road base") may serve the purpose, a graded gravel surface is really the minimum you need to ensure you never get stuck in mud or wind up with a pitted, rutted dirt access road. Asphalt is a big step up, offering improved structural integrity. Concrete is normally used only for driveways. Depending on the lay of the land, you may have to add drainage tiles or other runoff solutions to your budget.

- **Services.** Where will your preferred property lot be located, and how far from the road will it be placed? Whether you can connect to municipal water supply and sewer will radically impact your building budget. If those services aren't available,

you'll have to budget for drilling a well and installing a septic system. You'll also need power. The local power company must run a power line from the road to the home site. The power company usually charges by the linear foot (.30 m). Buried lines will cost more but are a good investment if your area experiences tornadoes or other severe weather events. Don't forget about internet connection. Remote locations mean that standard internet service may be expensive and even unavailable. You may need an alternative, such as a satellite dish for internet and TV.

- **Financing.** Not all mortgage companies and banks are on board with the barndominium trend. Look into the financing sooner rather than later. Although you may be able to secure a new-build mortgage, you may have to get creative. For instance, some barndominium owners who plan to use part of the structure for work have financed the structure through the FHA, as a farm loan.

- **Insurance.** Like finance companies, not all insurers have come around to the barndominium way of thinking. But as with any large investment, you'll need insurance. And you'll need to know how much it costs before you start building. Given how safe and stable these buildings are, insurance should be lower per square foot (.30 m) than with a traditional home.

- **Resale.** It is never wise to build a new home with the intention to move out of it soon. That is even truer for barndominiums. Although they offer a host of benefits to the aficionado, other potential home buyers may not see the value. Consequently, reselling a barndominium can take more time than selling a traditional home. If you're looking to build and flip, this isn't the structure for you.

Building a barndominium is no small project. Go into the process clear-eyed, with insight into all that the construction involves. That's the role of this book—to inform and enlighten potential barndo owners and head off unfortunate surprises. Barndominiums are a lifestyle as much as a physical structure. Get ready to claim that way of life!

Gallery of Barndominiums

Barndominiums follow the form of the simplest, most functional of buildings. But even though a barn has its own beauty, barn-inspired structures don't have to all look the same. In fact, barndominium designers and manufacturers have used the basic dimensions of this blocky rectangular farm mainstay as a jumping-off point to create a fabulous assortment of designs and styles. They have proven that it's possible to create eye-catching structures based on extremely basic inspiration. Simply adding an overhang with an outdoor seating area can transform the appearance of a barndominium. And there is so much more you can do.

Barndominium styles continue to evolve. Once a simple rectangular building with a shallow sloped roof and limited overhangs, a barn can look modern with a shed roof, or more like a traditional home, with a highly pitched roof.

The basic style leans toward smaller windows and a traditional barn door, but you can play around with those signature elements. Some barndo owners choose to fill one gable-end wall with floor-to-ceiling windows to open up an incredible view. Others use the barn doors as a distinctive entryway, a decorative feature, or easy access for an integral garage or workshop (or all three!).

The options vary tremendously and don't stop at the exterior. Almost any home style can be re-created inside a barndominium shell. The structure lends itself naturally to a farmhouse interior, with wood cabinetry and accents, and overstuffed, comfortable furnishings.

But you can go in a different direction entirely. From mid-century modern to contemporary, the interior of a barndominium is remarkably adaptable. This photo gallery illustrates the range of design potential for anyone jumping into the barndo life. That said, your imagination is really the only limitation when it comes to designing your dream barndominium.

Even a small barndominium can be a jaw-dropping structure with a little dressing up. This relatively simple barndo has a small footprint, but packs a huge visual punch thanks to twin cupolas, a copper roof and overhangs, and a sharp color scheme that breaks up neutral walls with pops of bright white doors, outdoor furnishings, and posts.

Gallery: EXTERIORS

LEFT: Exploit 3D rendering to preview the look. This is an ideal way to "see" your barndo complete before you ever commit to buying anything. Beautiful images like this capture the allure of any potential home in stunning detail. This technology allows you to easily make changes, from the building's color, to the style of the entryway, to the number and size of windows. More and more manufacturers are offering 3D rendering as part of their design services.

BELOW: Make a powerful first impression. Stacked stone accents, front doors with divided lights, country-style sconces, and a row of windows give this steel structure a homey feel.

Create a homey feel with traditional elements. Add features that transform the structure into a true "home." Here, a brick fireplace chimney makes a plain two-tone brown steel structure look more welcoming. It clearly signals that what lies inside is not farm equipment.

Go wild with your barndo. This simple but well-appointed home sits in a wildflower meadow, with a view to the east to take in brilliant sunrises. Carefully consider siting and positioning of the structure to achieve your ideal barndominium. The siting choice also has practical applications, such as the best orientation for roof-mounted solar panels.

LEFT: Indulge the potential of a custom design. This trim two-story gem shows the potential inherent in a barndominium's architectural form. The jaw-dropping gable wall of windows looks fantastic from the outside and even better on the inside. This type of feature adds significant cost but can make living in the space more enjoyable.

RIGHT: Small doesn't mean boring. Even though this barndominium is modestly sized, it packs a powerful visual punch. The look is embellished with wrought iron wagon wheels, timber overhang posts, and hanging baskets of seasonal flowers. These are easy ways to dress up a smaller home.

BELOW: Scintillate with stone. Stone naturally accents the look of steel barndominiums. An informal stacked stone waist and overhang post piers complement the simple, crisp lines of this two-story barndo.

Turn to timber for detailing. This timber-framed barndominium clearly shows why some homeowners are willing to pay more for a timber structure. Details like the cupolas and gable cutouts lend a distinctive character to the structure and go far beyond the simple barn form.

Power up the patio. Adding an L-shaped patio and overhang adds little cost or construction time, but injects style and a shaded, cool outdoor sitting and storage area. A large wraparound patio like this one is a wonderful way to take advantage of an eye-catching view.

A majestic barndo calls for statement garage doors. Here, a sleek, modern structure is perfectly complemented with unusual and unique garage doors formed of reclaimed planks run horizontally. Custom elements like this can be design focal points that put the entire home over the top.

Custom windows can be the focal points of a barndo's exterior look. This handsome home was designed with the rustic detailing and natural colors perfectly suited to the forested surroundings. The custom, peaked, twin gable-end windows are the stars of the show, not to mention expanding the light penetration and view from inside the home.

Mix and match for attention-grabbing effect. These typical barn doors have been fitted with mullioned windows that show off the chandelier fixtures inside. The symmetrical approach to window placement and the spacing of the decorative cupolas work especially well with the barn structure.

Soften metal siding with wood. As the overhang and faux shutters on this barndo illustrate, wood accents, details, and add-ons warm up the look of a steel barndominium. These flourishes also make the home more distinct and personal to the owner.

Accent with stone. Stone design elements inside and out partner naturally with barndominium look and style. Here, a stone knee wall lines the side of a large barndo, adding visual interest without overinflating the budget.

Capture the Wild West. The pioneer spirit and evocative look of a timber barndominium carry a special appeal. Many people feel that the fine craftsmanship and warmth of wood are well worth the higher price tag. Details such as the barn doors on either side of the entry make this structure stand out even amid spectactular natural vistas.

Gallery: INTERIORS

Play the slope. A naturally sloped barndominium ceiling is a distinctive feature. Although some homeowners install a flat ceiling in upstairs rooms, that negates the interesting, vaulted angle that adds character overhead.

Leverage the variety of wood marks and graining. If you've opted for a timber-framed barndominium like this one, make the most of wood's inherently appealing nature by using different woods in a variety of finishes. A plank floor and quarter-sawn timbers overhead contrast the more polished surfaces of wood cabinetry. The entire space is warm, welcoming, and visually interesting.

Let the space speak. Many barndominium owners design their interiors to exploit the often large open spaces within the shell. This room is a perfect example. Vaulted ceilings, double rows of sizeable windows, and a carefully furnished open floor plan create a feeling of free and open spaciousness. On the practical side, this type of layout and design also offers the unimpeded flow of natural light and fresh air.

Turn to wood for warmth and quiet. The wood-paneled walls in this great room hark back to traditional barn interiors, and also dull sound transmission, sometimes an issue with steel barndominiums.

Maintain the barn-style inspiration. Even if you've chosen a contemporary interior design, like this bedroom, you can still capture the charm of a barndo by using traditional architectural features. Here, sliding barn doors for the primary bath and faux exposed beams add hominess and authentic character to an otherwise neutral color scheme and sedate décor.

Define by function. Although wide-open floor plans are popular among barndominium owners, there's a good argument to be made for creating dedicated areas for specific purposes. Here, a distressed wood divider wall supports a TV and soundbar in an entertainment center, anchored by a U-shaped sectional sofa. The wall serves as an aesthetic feature, and clearly marks the function of this part of the floor plan.

Reinterpret classic elements. The barn door is an integral visual and functional element of barns and barndominiums, and a key indicator of the building style. But you don't have to use a wood barn door. Barndos regularly incorporate interior sliding barn doors redesigned to fit a specific interior style. Here, the door has frosted glass windows that suit the subtle and sophisticated interior design and provide some privacy.

Mix and match for visual interest. A timber-frame barndominium already packs plenty of dynamic appeal in the various textures of wood. But the interior is made even more interesting with the addition of a combination of textures and forms, as used in this kitchen and living room combination space.

Gallery: SAMPLE FLOOR PLANS

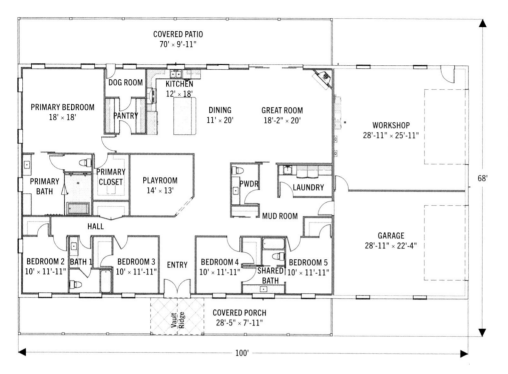

This floor plan illustrates just how much can be packed into the often cavernous interior of a large barndo. This particular home includes a spacious workshop and garage, making it the ultimate all-in-one structure.

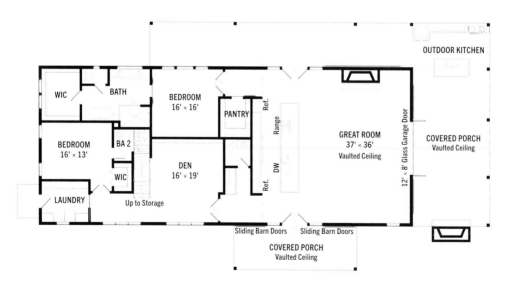

Embrace ease of design with a single story. As this plan shows, you can pack a lot into one story with careful design and planning. This gracious residence includes an outdoor kitchen and spacious great room. The single-floor construction is less expensive and ensures that homeowners can age in place, even if they develop mobility issues.

Go vertical for a large family. This large and dynamic two-story floor plan includes a space of their own for all family members. Thoughtful features like a laundry chute make sure that the home is as efficient and easy to live in as it is impressive in scope.

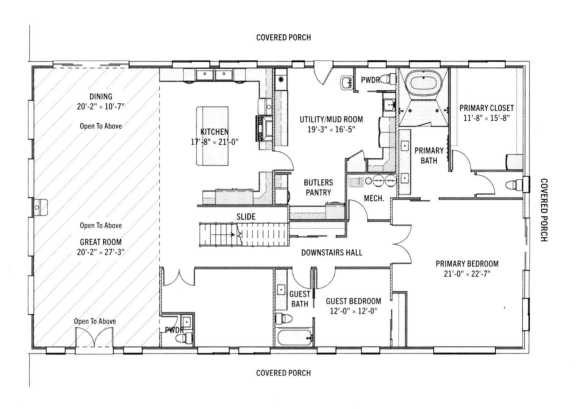

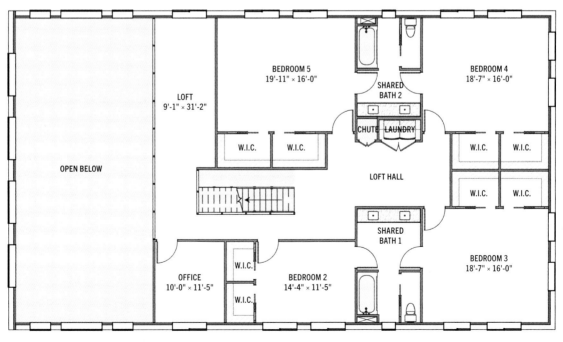

1 Barndominium Planning and Preparation

If you've read this far, you have a good idea of what a barndominium is, what types are available, and the inherent design potential. Now it's time to dig deeper and investigate the process of pulling the trigger and building your own perfect barndo.

MONEY MATTERS

A barndominium is a significant investment, just as any home is. It is likely one of the biggest purchases you'll make in your life. It's essential that you begin the process by considering your financial resources carefully. From there, you can establish a realistic budget and secure the financing you'll need. Here's the game plan:

1. WHAT CAN YOU AFFORD?

That's a tricky question. The answer hinges on basic math and a few intangibles. Start with what is known as debt-to-income ratio (DTI). Almost every lender will use this in deciding whether to extend a loan. The ratio is simply the amount of total debt payments you make each month, as a percentage of your gross (pretax) income. Those payments include car loans, general consumer loans, student loans, and credit card payments.

A common maximum recommended debt-to-income ratio is 40 percent. That means that no greater than 40 percent of your gross income goes to debt payments. But many lenders and mortgage companies often consider this ratio a bit too high.

A more traditional formula that banks and other financial institutions use is the "28–36 rule." This dictates that debt payments should not exceed 28 percent of gross income, and that *all* monthly household expenses (e.g., debt, food, rent, utilities, etc.) should not exceed 36 percent of your gross income. This is a conservative formula. This logic allows for a modest financial cushion against unexpected expenses. Those are the basic numbers, and are easy to calculate. Here's an example:

Gross monthly income:	$3,600
28 percent allowable DTI (multiply by .28)	×.28
	= $1,008
Current debt payments	- $192
Potential barndo loan payment	= $816

Many lenders will consider a higher debt-to-income ratio, up to and possibly beyond 40 percent. Several factors influence their decision, such as the tax deductibility of mortgage interest payments.

Lenders also take other factors into account when considering a loan application. For instance, not all monthly debt payments are the same. A student loan is a pure debt obligation. A car loan payment is secured by the equity in the vehicle. Those are different types of credit. A high credit card interest rate means you're paying off far less of the principal—and will take far longer to pay off any balance—than you would with a much lower interest rate.

Other considerations include how much of your available credit you're using, the amount of liquid savings you have available, and your credit score.

2. WHAT FACTORS INFLUENCE BARNDOMINIUM FINANCING?

Financing barndominium construction can be a challenge, more so than securing a mortgage on a traditional home. Determine if you can secure financing before proceeding with the process, especially if you're designing, planning, and building the structure. Financing a new build—barndominium or otherwise—is always a more complex process than getting a loan for an existing structure. Most people who have built their own dream barndominiums would say that the result more than justifies the effort.

Here are key factors that affect financing, and what types of loans you'll likely qualify for:

- **Comparable properties.** Lenders determine value by looking at the real estate market and reviewing prices for homes like the structure you're proposing to build or buy. They consider lot size, the structure's square footage, architectural style, and layout. Lenders can review the data of other local barndominiums, if there are any. If you're building the first barndominium in your area, financing may be slightly more challenging.

- **Local codes and regulations.** Barndominiums sometimes fall into a regulatory gray area with local building departments. For instance, some inspectors aren't quite sure whether a barndominium needs to meet residential codes, commercial codes, or both. This can make financing more complex. Determine where you want to build and investigate the code situation there.

- **Property factors.** The lending process will be easier if you've already bought the property, especially if water, sewage, and power services already exist. Lenders will want to know if the land has been cleared and prepared for construction, or if that work still needs to be done. They will also investigate the accessibility of the site; if there are environmental concerns, such as the presence of endangered species, or potential heavy metals contamination, and if there are any neighborhood restrictions imposed by local organizations like an HOA.

- **Down payment.** As with any home, the size of the down payment as a percentage of the entire project cost will influence not only whether you can get a loan, but also the terms of any loan.

The road to your dream barndominium likely runs through a financial institution.

Dreaming of a distinguished large barndominium like this? Be aware that potential lenders may not find comparable properties in the area.

3. WHAT ARE THE FINANCING OPTIONS?

Building your ideal new barndominium will require more creative financing than buying an existing structure would. Any financing you qualify for will generally require significantly more information and legwork.

Banks and lending institutions often don't have experience with unique homes. It can be difficult for them to assess risk and value, and some companies won't make loans for nontraditional homes such as barndominiums. A financial institution wants to know that it can easily resell the property should you default. Lenders follow established loan program guidelines and aren't particularly good at painting outside those lines.

If you're buying a barndominium kit, inquire about financing with the manufacturer. Some builders and barndominium manufacturers offer financing, typically short term, and limited to the structure, the construction, or both. They also may know which lenders in the local area finance barndos. Investigate traditional lenders such as banks and credit unions, and, if you strike out, national mortgage companies.

The downside to that type of financing is that homeowners incur additional fees when they take out a longer-term traditional mortgage. One way of avoiding those fees is a construction loan that naturally converts to a more traditional long-term mortgage as soon as the project is completed. Here are the most common types of financing for new barndominium projects:

- **New construction loan.** If you already own the property, are realizing a windfall profit from a home you're selling, have a large nest egg available in liquid funds, or you are enjoying a healthy salary, you may decide to take a loan that covers only the barndominium construction (or the cost of the prefab building itself with the construction). This type of loan typically has a shorter term than a mortgage, a year or less, and often higher interest rates. Loan funds are also typically doled out according to predefined stages, and hinge on proof of completion of each construction phase. Keep in mind that many steel barndominium manufacturers take a deposit up-front (typically 25 to 30 percent), with the balance due upon delivery to the job site.

- **Construction-to-Permanent (C2P).** This loan begins as construction financing and then converts into a traditional mortgage. The homeowner pays interest only until the construction is completed. These loans are often but not always more expensive than a traditional mortgage. Compare prices extensively to get the best rates.

- **Traditional fixed-rate mortgage.** This is a less common option for new barndominiums. A few banks and lenders such as Fannie Mae do offer new-construction, fixed-rate, long-term mortgages. The requirements are a high bar, and include a detailed budget, appropriate permits, an in-depth schedule, and much more. It's wise to prepare all of that anyway. The rates can be attractive, however.

A simple yet impressive single-story barndo can be a great baseline comparable property for your new build. This one is built along the lines of any prefab "kit" you might find through area manufacturers.

- **Farm loans.** You read that right. Considering the agricultural roots of this architectural style, it should come as no surprise that the U.S. Department of Agriculture will sometimes offer financing. If you qualify for a USDA loan, it may include 100 percent financing at an attractive rate.

- **FHA or VA loans.** The Federal Housing Authority and the Department of Veteran Affairs offer a smaller number of loans than other sources. Both types are worth looking into because of their low rates. You must be a veteran of military service to qualify for a VA loan. FHA financing is traditionally granted to individuals who might not qualify for a traditional mortgage because of their insufficient down payments, income, or credit scores. Typically, these loans require a 3.5 percent down payment and an extremely low debt-to-income ratio.

Once you've determined the likeliest financing sources, put together a budget and the other details you'll need to apply.

4. LOCATION, LOCATION, LOCATION!

Even the most wonderful barndo is of little use without a place to put it. As with all real estate, the key to building your ideal barndominium starts with location.

With few exceptions, a rural or semi-rural location enhances the allure of barndominium living. These large structures fit better on a larger piece of land. The typical barndominium property is at least an acre. Lot size is balanced against other factors affecting the value of the property and the property's viability as a site for your barndominium. Consider these carefully for any potential property:

- **Topography and environment.** Has the amazing view got you hooked? That's inspiration enough to consider a piece of property, but the view isn't quite so sweet if you build your dream home in a flood plain.

  Asking the right questions at the local Cooperative Extension Service office and checking with the United States Geological Survey will go a long way (see Resources, page 186). Those sources can alert you to local tornado, earthquake, wildfire, and flood threats. They will help you make an informed choice before you put money down.

  Of course, there are more property concerns than the risks of extreme weather and catastrophic events. Any lot should also drain away from the potential build site. Note topographical features, like boulders or gullies, that may present challenges to site access and excavation. Impediments to grading a foundation, installing a driveway, or laying an access road can exponentially increase costs and time frame.

  Local government agencies may have records on property lots, including topographical maps and previous soil surveys. Ultimately, though, you should hire a soil engineer or geological engineer to survey the site and provide a comprehensive report.

- **Soil.** Soil condition is one of the most important factors regarding a potential barndominium site. It's essential to have the soil tested, and may be required for a building permit. Hire a soil engineer or request your builder or contractor hire one. Soil engineers test two main factors: soil composition and contaminants.

  Soils can be expansive (weak), or compactible (strong). Expansive soils drastically increase in volume as they absorb water, potentially shifting foundations or other structures like concrete

The nature of barndominium living begs a wide-open vista like this one, with unimpeded views in all directions. The bonus? Rural property like this is often less expensive than a lot inside a city or town would be.

driveways. They can erode significantly and are generally unstable. Compactible, or strong, soils stay relatively stable over time. This type of soil is ideal as a base for a barndo's foundation.

Soil engineers also test for contaminants. Depending on local industry and the history of the plot, the soil may contain toxic metals like lead or cadmium, or other potentially dangerous compounds such as arsenic or high levels of carcinogenic chemicals.

Any soil engineer you use should be licensed through the state and certified by the National Council of Examiners for Engineering and Surveying. Some geological engineers have been licensed and certified as soil engineers and will offer additional perspective on the suitability of the lot. In any case, the engineer will bore holes and take several soil samples from areas around the lot. The number of samples depends on lot size.

- **Services.** No matter what size or type of barndominium you choose to build, or where you build it, you'll need power, water, and sewer services. How those are supplied can radically affect construction budget and timeline.

» **Water.** The easiest and least expensive source of clean water is a municipal supply. If there is a water main close, a supply line can be run to the house. If there isn't, you'll have to drill a well.

The cost of drilling a residential well varies widely from state to state, averaging $25 to $65 per foot (.30 m) for a complete well (drilling, wiring and electrical, well shaft casing, mechanicals, and related hardware). The average depth of a residential well is 100 to 300 feet (30.5–91 m) and the average width is 6 inches (15 cm). The challenge is judging how deep you'll need to drill. Ask neighbors who have a well on their property or inquire with a local well-drilling company about common well depths in the area.

The company will be able to give you an estimate based on their experience in the area and knowledge of the local geology. Keep in mind, though, once they begin, they'll keep drilling until they hit reliable, potable water. The deeper the water, the more likely it is to contain significant amounts of minerals. That's why it's wise to budget for a water softener system, or a whole-house water filtration system.

Beautiful isolated properties, like this forested lot around a rural red barndominium, often don't have access to municipal water. Pressurized tanks are key to a well and are usually located in a basement in a conventional house. Because most barndominiums are built on slabs, the tanks are instead placed in the least obvious location.

» **Sewer or septic.** Here again, tapping into existing services is the best option. However, many municipalities do not service rural or semi-rural areas with sewer lines. In that case, you'll need a septic system. The national average septic system installation cost is $5,800, from a low of about $3,100 up to a high of $8,500. The system's size determines the cost, and size is dictated by the number of people and fixtures in the house.

Septic System Comparisons

There are two basic types of septic systems:

Anaerobic	Aerobic
▪ Bacteria breaks down waste without oxygen	▪ Uses oxygen to activate bacteria to break down waste
▪ Simpler (one tank)	▪ Quicker and more efficient breakdown of waste
▪ More common	▪ More complex (three tanks)
▪ Requires slope for drainage	▪ Much more expensive
▪ Requires good "percolation" (rapid soil absorption)	▪ Works on flat ground
	▪ Doesn't require efficient percolation

Because these power poles run alongside this property, it cost less to connect the barndo than if they were further away (interruption to the view notwithstanding). Notice that the structure has been oriented so that the main windows avoid a view of power lines.

» **Power.** Running power to a home can be a challenge in any outlying area, but especially to a new build site. More than any other factor, this may affect the decision to choose or reject a potential barndominium site. The closer the property is to a main road, the less expensive it will be to connect to the local power grid. Sites far from a road or power pole incur significant expense.

The first step is to determine which power company serves the lot. This may not be immediately clear. Check the closest power poles for identification or call the government offices for the jurisdiction in which the lot falls and ask them which power company provides service to the area. Then schedule a site inspection.

An engineer will check the lot and decide the best way to connect the power. If a line needs to be run to the lot, the engineer assesses the most direct route. In some cases, that will be an overhead line to the barndo's power head. Other situations may require burying power lines. Either involves another permit and inspection.

Once you have the estimate from the power company, you can add that to your overall construction budget. Because the connection involves so many variables, the cost of a new power line can run from a few hundred dollars to several thousands.

Power companies are bureaucracies, and new power requests can easily languish on a desk or fall through the cracks. If you're on the clock to make a purchase decision, follow up with the power company regularly until you're given a detailed estimate. Get everything in writing.

» **Internet and TV.** Local internet providers often serve rural sites quite well. Although you will likely have to pay for a new hookup, which could run several hundred dollars, reliable service is usually well worth the one-time connection expense.

However, some locations aren't serviced by local providers. The alternative is a satellite dish provider. Internet service through a satellite is less reliable and consistent but where it's the only option, it's a good one.

As beautiful as they can be, rural locations are often served by only a small handful of first responders. It's wise to check what resources are available locally.

- **Title and rights.** These are issues that many potential property buyers aren't even aware could be problems. The good news is that in most cases, they won't be. But property rights that extend to other parties, or issues with the property title, may be deal breakers.

First check that the property is zoned for residential building. If it is zoned commercial, you'll need to apply for a variance to build a barndominium. That's not only time and effort, but it also complicates the process and delays the project. Occasionally, a variance is denied.

So, head to the local building department as soon as you find a piece of property. Ask if there are building restrictions for the property, due to the presence of an endangered species. The Endangered Species Act is federal legislation that can affect private property, and rural areas are more likely to harbor endangered species. Check with the local county extension service office for additional information.

Next, check the local municipality's records department to see if mineral or water rights are owned by someone other than the property owner. Rural property owners strapped for cash sometimes sell mineral and even water rights. You don't want to build your dream barndominium only to wake up one morning with a noisy nickel mine or natural gas drilling rig ruining your view, and possibly fouling your well-water source.

Lastly, have a title search done to determine if there are any liens against the property.

- **Access and jurisdiction.** Investigate if the property falls into an incorporated or unincorporated area. Municipal police, fire, and EMT services serve incorporated areas. Unincorporated areas have fewer resources: a sheriff's department, and a fire department on contract, or a volunteer firefighting force. Unincorporated areas sometimes have slower emergency response times. Although emergency services may not be a concern, it's worth knowing who supplies the services in your area. If you have children, determine which school district the property lies within.

5. HIRE A BUILDER
OR DO IT YOURSELF?

Finding the perfect location for your new barndominium is no small achievement. You've taken your first step toward becoming a barndominium owner. Now it's time to decide how you're going to get your new home built.

Most people turn to an experienced builder because barndominiums are unique structures. Proficiency with this type of construction can head off many problems. Experienced pros tend to do the job as efficiently and cost-effectively as possible. A contractor or builder are not, however, your only options.

Steel post-frame barndominium manufacturers fabricate the components for each given structure as a "kit," complete with detailed assembly instructions. If you are a highly skilled do-it-yourselfer, you can reasonably consider building your own barndominium, especially if you have friends or family who are skilled in the building trades. Obviously, a custom structure such as a timber-framed barndominium requires a craftsman's skills and should be left to a professional.

You can also serve as your own general contractor, an increasingly popular option. This involves double-checking credentials and references, hiring subcontractors, and making sure you have a complete, highly detailed punch list so that nothing falls through the cracks. It also involves dealing with any headaches that pop up, but ensures you control the process and can maintain a tight grip on schedule and expenses.

Doing it yourself involves an incredible amount of time, energy, and focus. Be honest with yourself before committing. You should be a high-energy, persistent personality. You'll also need patience. It's a big plus if you naturally look at problems as interesting and invigorating challenges, rather than frustrating headaches. You should be comfortable with confrontation because you may have to face down a subcontractor at some point. Lastly, details are everything. If you are disorganized, don't act as your own contractor.

Even a DIY option involves subcontracting out parts of the process. You'll want professionals to lay the foundation, plumb, wire, and run the HVAC. Still, doing much of the basic construction yourself can save quite a bit of money, and offers a sense of pride in craftsmanship.

A Builder Versus a Contractor

There are many ways to work with a company or individual professionals to build a barndominium. If you have a builder custom design the structure, you'll likely use that pro to construct it. If, on the other hand, you're buying a prefab package, you'll need a local builder or contractor. Suppliers often provide referrals to local pros they have verified. It's important to use professionals who have deep experience working with barndominiums.

A turnkey solution—one company to do everything, from design services, to permitting, to laying the foundation and ultimately building the barndo—is the easiest, least stressful option. Although more expensive, it's the route many potential barndominium owners take.

A general contractor can assemble a prefab steel post-frame kit. That pro can subcontract site prep and laying the slab foundation, along with plumbing, electrical, and other services, and will deal with permits and permissions.

Be aware that the more you compartmentalize project tasks, the more likely it is for something to fall through the cracks. For instance, it's a common mistake for someone acting as his or her own contractor or using a general contractor to fail to arrange for offloading components from a delivery truck. Contractors won't necessarily realize that they need to have heavy equipment onsite to offload components.

Using a general contractor still offers the chance to negotiate doing some of the work yourself. If you want to tackle a task like painting steel trusses, work with your professional to accommodate that in the punch list and schedule. Most builders, on the other hand, understandably avoid owner participation; there is too much potential for the novice to compromise the work or hold up the project.

Any building professional should be licensed and insured. Make sure everything is in writing. Draft a detailed contract explicitly spelling out schedule, payment stages and due dates, method of payment, and events that would cause payments to be withheld. Plainly lay out how expenses that exceed the budget will be handled.

The installation of a metal roof, especially one involving dormers, hips, valleys, or other unusual features, is a dangerous and exacting task best left to seasoned professionals.

This is a matter of being reasonable and protecting all parties. You don't want a contractor or builder switching to more expensive windows simply because he dragged his feet on ordering windows and the units originally specified are no longer available. On the other hand, if you add a skylight or a more elaborate front door at the eleventh hour, the professional shouldn't have to eat the additional installation cost.

Building a barndominium is no small undertaking. The more you plan and troubleshoot problems in advance, the more you ensure a smooth building process and a successful build. Whether you do some of the work or not, it's wise to understand the process. That starts with design, and you'll find all you need to know about that topic in the next chapter.

Managing a Contractor

Whether you decide to use a builder or contractor, a little advance troubleshooting goes a long way. You're likely to get stung most by the questions or issues you didn't think to consider. These points are especially worthy of your attention if you're acting as your own general contractor.

- **Account for add-ons.** If you've made any last-minute custom changes to a prefabricated "kit" barndominium, that may change the contractor's role and costs. For instance, bigger or more windows will increase installation time and labor. Not only should you expect this to increase the quoted contractor cost, you also need to be sure to notify the contractor elements, so that they can adjust the project schedule.

- **Site access.** Moving heavy equipment, or just overloaded work pickup trucks, to and from a possibly remote build site may be a challenge. Make sure that your contractor or builder has assessed the routes of access to the site, and that you won't be surprised by any roadway work that could hold up the schedule and add to the budget. This is even more of an issue if you're acting as your own contractor. It's something many homeowners haven't dealt with and can easily be a problem when subcontractors start trying to access the build site to work on their parts of the project. If you're the contractor, ask one or more of the professionals you'll be using to visit the site and provide feedback on accessibility.

- **Determine the reasons why.** Don't be afraid or overwhelmed to query your contractor on the reasoning behind different decisions. For instance, many contractors go the slightly more expensive route of using 2 × 8 joists throughout, when codes often allow 2 × 6s in some locations. By keeping the joists the same depth everywhere, the second floor surface—even if it's just used for storage—remains even. Greater joist width also allows for larger ductwork (and potentially less of it) to be run between floors. Small decisions like this can make future changes and adjustments during the building process easier.

Gallery: OUTDOOR ESCAPES

Abundant space is a hallmark of many barndominium interiors, but it's just as often a feature of the surrounding outdoor space. Given that many barndominium locations are isolated and enjoy abundant privacy, well defined outdoor living areas are a natural, and key to enjoying all that barndominium life offers.

Extend services to a firepit for convenience. The gas firepit here is fed by a plumbed gas line that makes impromptu outdoor social sessions easy and simple. It also avoids the clean-up and wood hauling that a wood-burning firepit would entail. It's an excellent option in localities where a plumbed gas line is possible.

Tub your barndo deck. A hot tub is an ideal addition to a barndominium side deck, especially where there is a view like this forested landscape. The composite deck shown here is low maintenance, and placing the tub right next the wall of the kitchen ensures that it's easy and inexpensive to plumb. This promises many wonderful nights of stargazing in hot-water splendor.

Create the outdoor space that suits you. Although most barndominiums exploit rural or semi-rural locations with wide open expanses left largely wild, that doesn't mean you have to. The barndominium owner here has decided to opt for the more conventional suburban backyard, with a lawn and tidy fence. The fence ensures that family pets can be let out without worry that local wildlife might pose a threat, and the sod ensures a comfy surface underfoot for barefoot outdoor relaxing.

Isolate an outdoor kitchen for a special entertaining area. With all the space around most barndominiums, it's often easy to set aside an outdoor area separate from the main building, creating a special entertaining area. This one features a barbecue grill set into a counter, tiered deck design, and a heater for cold forest nights.

Optimize outdoor living by creating a four-season space. Good weather or bad, this custom structure ensures that the group can gather under a stable roof and enjoy a family meal outside. The addition of a firepit allows for distinct groupings and conversation areas during family or social get-togethers.

Keep outdoor entertaining close for convenience. This firepit is protected by a gable-end overhang and sits outside a door leading into a great room and kitchen. It's an incredibly handy location spurring spontaneous enjoyment of the outdoor location and drinks by a crackling fire.

2

Design Your Perfect
Barndominium

The design process is when your new barndominium home starts to become a tangible reality. Design involves sifting through both needs and preferences, envisioning the physical footprint and interior layout. This stage is undeniably enjoyable. However, it calls for careful consideration and a laser-like focus on details.

First decide who will do the design. A few prefab manufacturers offer design services, including interior floor plans through stamped blueprints. More commonly, steel building companies don't create the foundation plan or stamped interior floor plans. Usually, another source will create them for you, or you will do them yourself, before applying for building permits.

A handful of designers work specifically on barndominiums (meet one of them in Case Study on page 70). Many builders offer design services. If you're just a little tech-savvy, you can design your own barndo using one of the many high-powered design programs available.

Regardless, think of design as a funnel. Start with the biggest decisions, like how large the building will be and how many windows and doors it will have. Then work down to the floor plans of individual rooms. Generally, the process requires that form follow function.

SIZE AND SHAPE

Any barndominium's footprint is intimately intertwined with the interior floor plan. That means whether you're sifting through the limited options of a prefab kit or looking at the unlimited possibilities of a purely custom barndo, you must keep both exterior and interior considerations in mind, because they work together.

Barndominium footprints are defined by width, length, and height. Those factors determine the size, outline, and complexity of the engineered slab foundation for almost all barndominiums. Barndominium size and shape also determine usable interior square footage.

Some prospective owners build fully custom barndominiums. That allows you to determine precisely how big the home will be, what shape it will take, and what exterior detailing it will have. Take this path and you'll be limited only by codes and accepted practices, your imagination, and what you're willing to pay. Custom barndominiums also require a skilled designer; they are not DIY design projects.

Most of us have a more modest budget. Fortunately, barndominiums offer the perfect economical home. Even if you can't afford to create a unique barndo from the ground up, you'll still be able to choose from a wealth of sizes and shapes among available prefab kits. Some are L- or T-shaped, but most are simple rectangles. The less complex the structure, the less money you'll spend. Most manufacturers offer some level of customization, should you want to make a few changes to your preferred model.

Although this overhang that covers the L-shaped patio seems like a simple construction, it is essential that both the patio and roof be included in the site plan to ensure proper prepartion of the building's footprint.

A rectangular footprint need not determine the visual nature of the building. Here, the traditional shape serves as the base for a visually powerful asymmetrical roof line. The overall shape of the building creates captivating interior spaces as well.

A large barndo like this requires exceptional planning to build a weathertight shell that is still energy efficient even with two window walls, and with a driveway contiguous to the foundation slab.

Here are common prefab kit sizes and their respective raw square footage measurements. "Raw square footage" represents the completely empty floor space inside, with no interior framing elements in place. The more walls in your floor plan, the more square footage you lose.

Typical Barndominium Kit Sizes	
Footprint (W × L)	Raw Square Footage/ Meters
30 × 40 ft. (9 × 12 m)	1,200 (108)
40 × 60 ft. (12 × 18 m)	2,400 (216)
40 × 75 ft. (12 × 23 m)	3,000 (276)
50 × 75 ft. (15 × 23 m)	3,750 (345)
60 × 60 ft. (18 × 18 m)	3,600 (324)
60 × 70 ft. (18 × 21 m)	4,200 (378)

A simple rectangular shape like this one is the easiest to design and build. An interesting color combination, covered wrap-around patio, and lush landscaping ensure that this home is anything but boring.

Not just interior walls, but appliances, storage, and other features cut into usable square footage. In the case of post-and-beam or any timber-frame kit, the framing members themselves may reduce the available living space.

You can add square footage to barndominiums by going vertical. Choose a barndominium 20 feet (6 m) high or higher, and you can frame out a loft or even an entire second floor. That can potentially nearly double your available square footage.

Gallery: TRULY GREAT ROOMS

The cavernous space inside many barndominiums opens up the potential for a stunning great room as center point for the rest of the floor plan. Great rooms aren't limited to barndominiums, but barndos have redefined this type of space. Implemented correctly, a great room ties together the entire interior layout, fostering interaction, and making for incredible and unique interior looks.

Flaunt precision timber framing. Going to the extra expense to have an engineered timber-frame barndo built? Might as well show off all the framing elements and joinery. This home even reveals the roof purlins. It's a visually busy look with something of interest from every vantage point, and the comforting warmth of wood pervading the interior.

Create conversation pits. A great room with a vaulted ceiling and ample floor space can easily become a large, impersonal area that lacks character. The way to prevent that is to define social interaction areas within the larger floor plan to create intimacy and a sense of coziness.

Facilitate flow. One of the most wonderful aspects of designing your barndominium around a great room is that the space becomes a natural anchor for the floor plan. It's especially effective for open floor plans like the one in this stately barndo interior, where the layout encourages social interaction between rooms and allows for maximum light and air flow.

Choose a focal point. Given that a barndo great room often serves many purposes, it's wise to design around a focal point. In this room, it's the fireplace. The seating group centers on that feature, and the media center next to it is accessible as well. The focal point helps define the area and adds character to the room.

Complement the room with the right couches. Couches are often anchor pieces of a furniture suite and no more so than in a great room. Undersized couches will "float" in the room and look odd. The right couches have enough visual weight to match soaring ceilings, window walls, and abundant floor space.

Let the room breathe. Great rooms are meant to be spacious. Crowding the room with furniture diminishes the perception of space. The balance of furnishings and space between different areas in the open floor plan of this barndominium allows the great room to actually be great. It's an open, airy, light-filled and attractive room design.

WHAT SQUARE FOOTAGE?

Few barndominium owners complain about having too much square footage. In fact, the potentially large interior spaces of these unique homes, at a smaller-than-normal cost per square foot, is one of the primary attractions.

- **Family matters.** When it comes to figuring out the space you need, the people who live in the barndominium are the most important consideration. The traditional formula for new home sizing is 600 square feet (56 sq m) per person. That means a family of three would look for 1,800 square feet (167 sq m), and four family members ideally require a 2,400-square-foot (732-m) structure.

That's a good starting point but factoring in the number of residents is not quite so simple. Families inevitably change. Couples become empty nesters as kids go off to college or start their own lives elsewhere. Will the space easily convert to a new interest like classic cars or horses? Would you leave the door open to kids moving back home?

You may also need or want more than average square footage if, for instance, one member of the family has special needs and requires accessibility features such as roll-under counters in bathrooms and extra-wide doorways.

It's wise to carefully consider a barndo kitchen in relation to the overall floor plan, because kitchens so often function as a social center in the home.

Although this barndominium has plenty of floor space, the height makes it seem even more spacious. In a two-story barndominium (or any over 18 feet [5.5 m.]), think vertically as well as horizontally.

Extra space may also be in your plans to meet future needs like an in-law unit for aging parents. Of course, you may just desire more room to spread out. Ultimately, pick a size that suits your family, your life, personal preference, and, of course, budget.

Case Study:
THE CREEK HOUSE REALIZED

Stacee Lynn is a barndominium designer, and owner of the design firm Our Barndominium Life (see Resources, page 186). She brings a unique perspective to her work because she literally lives the ideas and theories that drive her designs. She lives in one of her earliest creations, "The Creek House." The story of that design offers guideposts and ideas for any prospective barndo owner.

The Creek House design evolved from what was originally intended as a weekend getaway on a large plot of land surrounded by the Sam Houston National Forest. The more time Stacee and her husband, Oliver, spent revising the design, the more they realized that it could be their permanent home.

Like so many others, Stacee and Oliver were drawn to the allure of more elbow room, access to relatively private outdoor living areas, and a simpler, slower pace of life. The rural plot they bought was a tree-studded, isolated oasis of peace in a forest.

The first order of business was to determine the ideal building site and structural orientation. They decided on a placement roughly in the center of the lot. Stacee chose a north-facing orientation, as most new home builders do in the hot climate of southeastern Texas. Facing the home north or west leaves the front of the barndominium out of direct sunlight over the course of the hottest part of the day when the sun is the strongest.

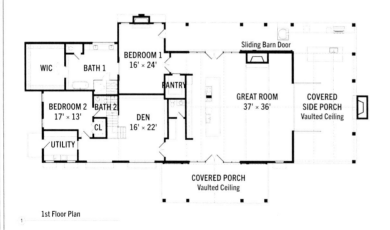

1st Floor Plan

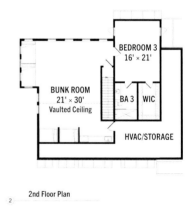

2nd Floor Plan

The Creek House floor plan, carefully laid out for maximum livability.

The Creek House's north-facing front porch/foyer.

Planning the Exterior

The Creek House site differed from those of many barndominiums, which so often get plunked down on bucolic flat plains, with wide open vistas and few if any trees in sight. Even after felling trees for the access road and the build site itself, the site was still surrounded by 80-foot (24-m) pines offering abundant shade.

- **Access.** Although many builders site a barndominium in as direct a line as possible from the closest road, Stacee literally took a different path. She chose a site that was essentially oriented in a dogleg from the main road. People entering the property drive through a copse of trees and then go left, where they are treated to the sight of the Creek House revealing itself majestically among the trees.

(continued)

The tree-studded property ensures wonderful views and heat-beating shade throughout the day.

- **Engineered foundation.** Stacee and Oliver took no chances with their foundation. The soil in the area is sandy loam, prone to extreme expansion and contraction in response to moisture and dryness. The Creek House foundation stays stable during soil shifting thanks to 30-inch-deep (76-cm) perimeter footings, 18-inch (46-cm) beams, and abundant use of heavy-gauge rebar throughout the slab. The foundation helps insure against a structural issue with a foundation down the road—a six-figure problem—not to mention that a structural issue could possibly compromise the building.

  As Stacee points out, "Your family sleeps there. You sleep there. The people you love are in that home." The takeaway is that simply thinking in terms of depth is not thinking clearly about the role a barndo foundation plays in the building, and the protection it provides.

Hard to tell where the Creek House interior ends, and this outdoor patio living area begins. Comfort, luxury, and beauty are the common elements that tie inside and outside together.

A wonderful outdoor kitchen and relaxing space, that can be used in any weather.

- **Outdoor living area.** Stacee and Oliver wanted to spend as much time outside as possible, enjoying the surroundings. She included an outdoor kitchen and sitting area to extend the indoor space. This outdoor "room" sees use almost every night. It is both an evocative and practical area of the home.

  The benefits are intangible, but important, and become clearer as Stacee describes how the space is used: "There is something relaxing about having my morning cup of coffee out there, with the dogs running around, as I think about what my day will be like. At the end of the day, my husband and I will head out there. I'll have a glass of wine and he'll have a bourbon. He'll be grilling steaks and we'll just relax, listening to our favorite music."

- **Exterior building elements.** Stacee leans toward awnings as both aesthetic and practical exterior elements. Awnings provide valuable shade for windows and areas facing the midday sun, where rake (eave) and gable extensions don't help as much.

  She is also a fan of cupolas, a decorative feature that naturally complements a barn-inspired structure. "Barndominiums have simple roof lines, which can be dressed up to give the barndo a little wow or pop. Cupolas do that beautifully and inexpensively."

  She is adamant about roof pitch and how it affects barndo appearance. In Stacee's book, more is better when it comes to pitch angle. The "pitch" is the number of inches of drop over a foot of roof span, depicted as relational (e.g., 3/12 [7.6/30 cm]). The higher the first number, the steeper and more dramatic the roof pitch. Traditionally, steel buildings have relatively shallow pitches: 2/12 (5/30 cm) or 3/12 7.6/30 cm). Shallow pitches are technically easier to fabricate. Stacee is of a different mind, saying, "I tend to design on a 6, 7, or 8/12 pitch. My barndo is 8/12. It produces a great residential look. Most of my clients don't want something like a 2/12 or 3/12 pitch, because it looks too industrial."

(continued)

Planning the Interior

The most basic decision is a single-story layout versus two stories, affecting the choice of building, and its height. Stacee's clients overwhelmingly prefer single-story barndominiums. A single story ensures the owner can age in place without concern for future mobility issues. It's a simpler layout and less prone to wasted areas, such as upstairs guest bedrooms that see little use.

Beyond this starting point, Stacee has developed time-tested, fundamental design principles.

- **Exploit unique architectural elements.** Stacee's design sense is to leave steel structural elements exposed. As part of the Creek House construction, she and her husband painted the steel trusses before they were installed. She sums up the feeling of many barndo owners, saying, "I think painted, exposed steel is sexy."

The Creek House great room. The combination of tin ceiling and exposed painted black steel trusses makes for an incredibly riveting visual.

A queen bunk in the grandkid's TV and bunkroom serves as comfortable seating before bedtime.

- **Start the floor plan with the biggest space.** You've figured out the building size and shape, exterior accents, outdoor areas, and indoor exposed features. Now it's time to put pen to paper and design your interior living space. But where to start? You can follow Stacee's lead and start with the largest space, the great room (spoiler alert: all her designs feature a great room). It's inevitably the largest piece in the design puzzle and a multi-purpose common space.

- **Navigate human interactions.** At the heart of every design Stacee tackles the question, "How will people interact in the space?" She offers the example of a client who needed to keep an eye on grandkids. "She wanted a bedroom that could also be a game room. It had to be downstairs, a bunkroom where her grandkids could play and where she could easily check on them. We created a beautiful set of glass barn doors that look into a bunkroom off the kitchen, with a TV and space for games and bunk beds. She could be entertaining, and still easily look into that room and check on her grandchildren."

  The point is always to consider the design through the lens of how the people in the home will relate to one another. Parents with young children might want to place a kids' bedroom right next to the primary suite, whereas parents of teens might position the bedrooms on opposite sides of the great room.

  Keep in mind that one of the best traits of barndos is that interior walls can come down and go up relatively easily. That means that it's not difficult to evolve a floorplan over time, to adapt to changing circumstances.

(continued)

The media and game room isolates the quiet bedrooms from noise.

- **Double duty instead of dead space.** Stacee's barn-dos are often large, but no space is wasted. Quite the opposite; almost every room serves multiple functions. Her floorplan mantra? "Design spaces to use every day. It costs too much to design, decorate, furnish, insure, keep cool, and keep clean spaces that you use only occasionally." Practicing what she preaches, her second bedroom is also a home gym used for daily workouts. The grandkids' bunk room? Also a TV room.

- **Ban the hallway.** Walk through the Creek House and you quickly discover its ease of movement and fluid traffic flow. Stacee achieves this by avoiding the use of hallways and other transitional spaces, saying, "I don't like hallways. I design pass-through rooms. I design a lot of combination rooms because they can do double or triple duty. I say let's make your front porch your foyer, and then you come straight into whatever the living space is."

  Not only does this approach make for ease of movement throughout Creek House (and all of Stacee's designs), but it also limits the impact of interior walls. As she points out, "Every time you add a wall, you're taking away usable square footage and you're adding cost. The Sheetrock, the lumber, the electrical. So, I use as few walls as possible."

- **Walk around your design.** Stacee's company offers the ability to digitally walk through the space prior to committing to the design. This can be a revealing exercise. Stacee has seen it change customers' decisions. "I designed a barndo for a client and the primary bathroom was a little tight. I said, 'Let us do a bumpout on the back of this.' She said, 'No, no, Stacee, I don't want to spend the money.' We did the 3D video, and I showed her. She said, 'Yeah, I get it now. Let's do the bumpout.' I could explain all I wanted, and I wasn't going to convince her. But that short video did."

- **Consider utility.** Barndominium owners don't just live in their spaces. One unique attraction is a barndo's suitability to place work and utility spaces side by side with living areas. Many floor plans incorporate hobby workshops, professional work-spaces, garages, or other utility areas.

Common Barndominium Utility Areas	
PURPOSE	**SPACE AND RATIONALE**
Garage	180 to 200 square feet (17–19 sq m) per car, on average. Modern pickups or luxury SUVs should be allotted closer to 220 (20 sq m). (Doesn't include room to turn around and maneuver.)
Woodworking Workshop	125 to 400 square feet (12–37 sq m) depending on whether the woodworker works with hand tools, or large power tools, as well as storage needed and ventilation equipment
Home Business	200 to 1,000 square feet (19–93 sq m), depending on shipping frequency, physical size of products, number of employees, and storage needs
General Workshop	300 to 600 square feet (28–56 sq m) depending on amount of hardware and number and size of tools
Motorcycle or Car Restoration (with Lift)	Motorcycle garage space should be at least 400 square feet (37 sq m); car garage space should be at least 576 (54 sq m). The more space, the better.
Stables (Two Horses)	1,200 square feet (30 × 40 ft. [111 sq m]). Stalls should be 196 square feet (18 sq m) (14 × 14 feet or 4.2 × 4.2 m) Can reduce square footage if there is stand-up storage above the stalls for hay, supplies, and equipment

The Garage Rules

A garage is perhaps the most common nonliving space included in the floor space of a barndominium. Although it's a natural use of the abundant space most barndos offer, it's wise to take a few steps to ensure what happens in the garage, stays in the garage . . . and doesn't affect the living space.

- **Account for noise.** Working on cars, motorcycles, or other vehicles or power equipment can be awfully noisy. If you anticipate that someone will be working in the garage while others are in the home, watching TV, or even sleeping, it will pay to limit sound transmission. To start with, many owners install a drop ceiling in the garage portion of their barndominiums. These can easily be installed with kits that include acoustic ceiling tiles. Incorporating soft surfaces in the space, such as wood cabinets and workbenches, will also help prevent sound from bouncing around or echoing. You can also construct the wall between the living space and garage as a sound dampening barrier itself. Use sound-deadening drywall, and soundproofing panels inside the wall, to limit sound transmission from once area to the other. If the wall is already built, you can invest in sound-dampening tiles or panels to cover the wall. Used in music studios, these can be quite effective and are an easy and effective post-construction solution—although they can be pricey.

- **Ensure air quality.** Exhaust from vehicles or power equipment can be toxic, especially when the garage door is closed due to cold outside temperatures. Where you'll be running engines inside, make sure you install "active" air venting or filtration. This means a motorized fan, rather than a simple vent. The fan should be rated for the cubic feet in the garage (cubic feet is calculated by multiplying length, by width, by height). This number is listed as the "CFM" of the fan.

- **Think through flooring.** Although it's acceptable to leave the concrete floor as it is, that may not be your best option. Dropped heavy equipment may mar the floor and make it less attractive. For additional protection and a potentially unique and more interesting surface, you can coat the floor with epoxy. Available in several different colors and "flake" versions, epoxies are easy to apply, durable, and easy to clean. If that solution is more effort than you want to put into the floor, consider aftermarket rubber tiles. These, too, are incredibly durable, can be laid in a couple of hours, and come in several different eye-catching appearances. Not only is a rubber garage floor cleanable, it also goes a long way toward limiting sound echoing and transmission in the barndo.

- **Size it right.** You'll find guidelines for garage size based on the number of vehicles, on the opposite page. However, home craftspeople rarely discover they have too much space. More is usually better. When initially designing the barndo, keep in mind the amount and type of storage you'll need, how many people will be working in the space at the same time, and how much room you'll have around the vehicles to maneuver something bulky, like an air compressor.

- **Positioning.** The actual position of your barndominium—the direction the building faces and where it's placed on the property—will have a big impact on other design decisions. The most obvious considerations are sunlight and heat.

Traditionally, builders orient a new home with the front door facing south. That's because in the northern hemisphere, the sun tracks through the southern sky, east to west. The front of a south-facing house will be brightly lit throughout the day and stay warmer than one facing north, a benefit in such places as Colorado, Oregon, or the Dakotas. Homeowners or builders in hotter climates, such as parts of Texas, Oklahoma, and Arizona, orient the front to the north, conserving energy and keeping the home cooler during the day.

Barndominium lots are typically large, and the front of the home is often arbitrary. Consequently, the side with the most windows is often positioned facing south (or north, depending on local climate).

However, the sun's path through the sky is more than just an east-to-west track. For instance, the sun is lower in the sky during winter. Build a barndo with a wall of south-facing picture windows in the summer, and you may be surprised in the winter when the sun creates glare and hot spots and shines right in your eyes as you relax in your living room.

Long daily exposure to harsh, direct sunlight can also fade upholstery, reflect blindingly off polished concrete floors, and quickly overheat an interior. That's why many people include overhangs or awnings for openings on south- and east-facing walls.

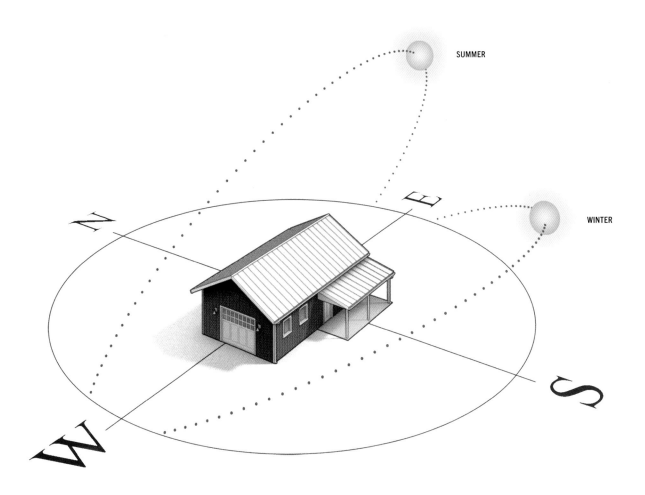

Sometimes, envisioning what an unbuilt barndo will be like in place involves interacting with the site itself

Before deciding on final barndominium positioning, understand how the sun tracks over the home site. Note how trees or nearby hills cast shade and shadows at different times during the day, and how shadows from the building itself will affect outdoor sitting areas.

Hoping to use solar power? That will influence barndominium positioning. Solar panels must be positioned facing south to be as efficient as possible, with sun exposure maximized. That usually means a long roof plane-oriented east to west.

Whatever company you choose to install the roof panels and electrical system will first do a solar site survey and suggest the best building orientation based on your roof pitch. You can see how the sun shines on your home site throughout the day with a sun-mapping app.

A lake view, or a clear line of sight to any body of water, makes for an impressive backdrop that should be seen as much as possible from the home.

- **Other site considerations.** Because barndominiums are so commonly placed on larger, rural plots, the best view can be an important site consideration. It only makes sense to orient the structure to enjoy the best possible view through the biggest windows.

A more mundane concern is placing your entry door facing the nearest paved road to lessen the expense of the access road or driveway and have it be closer to your house.

If you're acting as your own contractor, siting is going to be one of your first and most challenging decisions. In most cases, you'll be required to have the site professionally surveyed prior to construction, as part of local permitting requirements. Use the opportunity to consult the surveyor on the ideal home site and position.

You can also hire a builder or contractor to advise you on structure positioning and site development. Not only will seasoned pros have experience in the local area, but they will also be able to give you input on the appropriate foundation given the soil condition, the building, sun exposure, and other issues you might not think of.

On the other hand, if you've hired a builder or a general contractor, that professional will probably offer initial site consultation, design services, and plan drafting as part of his or her services.

EXTERIOR DESIGN

Besides the building shape, a barndo's exterior appeal depends most on the number and type of windows and doors, and the building's color. The ability to change window or door size and placement are where design tools and manufacturer's design templates come in handy. Whether the barndominium is timber-framed, pole barn construction, or a steel post frame, windows and doors cannot interfere with the structural integrity of the outer walls. Posts or poles must be placed at specific intervals to properly support the roof.

That's not to say you can't have that floor-to-ceiling, gable-end wall of windows you're dreaming of. You can. It will just take time, expertise, and expense. The more openings, the more expense. The following pages outline other major design factors to consider when envisioning the exterior of your barndo.

Most windows, and even the entryway, are more easily placed on the gable ends of a steel or timber-frame barndominium. The engineering needed to accommodate opening placement is much easier for gable walls than it is for side walls.

You don't need a gable-end wall of windows to make a spectacular impression. This attractive barndo includes modest stock windows strategically placed—complementing the gable door and detailing—to provide a view from the inside and a sharp look from the outside.

Multiple roofs on the same barndo create dynamic visual interest, especially if the building is an unusual shape, such as this L-shaped barndo. Notice that the roofs are all painted white: this increases energy efficiency and keeps the interior cooler in warm climates.

- **Roofs.** Traditional barns have a low pitch. Pitch is the amount of slope per foot, expressed as the inches of drop: 3/12 slopes 3 inches for every foot of roof width, or 7.6 cm. for every 30 cm. of roof. Residential barndominiums tend to have steeper pitches of at least 6/12 (15 over 30 cm). This creates a more dramatic, less commercial-looking building. However, the steeper the pitch, the less usable the space under the roof line.

Timber-frame and wood barndos with steeply pitched roofs may feature traditional asphalt shingle roofs and are sometimes clad with clapboard or other wood siding. But most new barndominiums have metal roofs and siding. Here are the types of roof panels used:

» **Continuous form metal roofing.** Also known as purlin-bearing rib panels (PBR) or corrugated roofing. These roofing panels completely overlap each other, yielding more metal-to-metal contact. That means this roof will be stronger and more weather tight. Continuous metal roofing is easier and quicker to install, and the least expensive. But it tends to look commercial and utilitarian.

» **Traditional standing seam.** Roofs with these panels installed correctly are "100-year roofs." Panels are prepped, then screwed to roof sheathing or purlins and trusses. Subsequent panels are attached to previous ones using clips. Once all are installed, they are seamed, securing each panel together by mechanically folding over the seams. This can be done by hand, but most pros use a power seamer. It has wheels and a motor and seams each pair of panels from eave to ridge, quickly, easily, and precisely. Eave ends are folded over to slip securely onto drip-edge guides.

» **Hidden fastener snap-lock seam.** These are the most common barndominium roof panels. They last as long as standing seam panels do. The panels interlock along a snap-lock seam that is easy to complete by hand. Panels are screwed down, and subsequent panels are hooked or slide up over the previous panel's ridge, and then pressed to lock together. This creates a squared-off rib, instead of the peaks of a standing seam.

A steeper roof, like the one on this small barndominium, lends drama and showcases elements like the distinctive roof color and cupolas here.

Seamed wall panels installed vertically is one of the most common barndominium looks, but far from the only way walls can be installed. This process and panel type maintains the lines of the metal roofing panels, drawing the eye down to the patio.

- **Walls.** Most new barndominiums use metal wall panels even if the framing is wood. That's because the panels will last an extremely long time, are durable, suit the look of the building style, and may never need repainting. They are also relatively inexpensive in relation to other wall cladding options, and are easy to install. Barndominium kit suppliers usually offer a limited variety of wall panel types and colors. Metal roofing suppliers offer a wider range of types:

» **Fastener style.** The first distinction is concealed versus exposed fasteners. Exposed-fastener wall panels install quicker and easier and cost less. However, the fasteners can be entry points for moisture and insects. Most homeowners find them unattractive.

A more traditional look, the panels on this barndo convincingly mimic clapboard siding, but with far longer lifespan and less maintenance.

» **Profiles.** There are many different panel profiles. Corrugated wall panels are the least expensive, and easiest to install. However, they are generally considered an industrial look. Board-and-batten profiles are more common and a traditional appearance. They look like a flat wall surface with boards attached at regular intervals. A flat profile is a modern, sleek look. It has thin gaps between panels. Wall panels can be run horizontally or vertically for different appearances.

Most wall-panel suppliers offer a range, from textured in a palette of colors, to simulated wood grain patterns. Wall-panel styles vary more than roof panel styles.

▪ **Windows.** Ordering a barndominium kit? Your choice of windows may have been made for you because many kits include both windows and doors. You can replace size for size if you want to increase R-value (see box on page 97) or would just prefer a different look. Suppliers often allow some changes or swaps. Even if they don't, you can order different windows to match, and install them in place of what would have been supplied.

Keep in mind that building codes may dictate window placement and usage. For instance, local codes comply with the International Residential Code, which calls for operable windows at least 5 square feet (0.5 sq m) in any bedroom. This is a safety concern, because windows are necessary in an emergency such as a fire.

Those restrictions are minimal, though. The truth is window openings are not standardized home to home. There is an astonishing range of options. Some practical issues, such as frame material, will impact price, durability, and visual appeal. Other factors are purely aesthetic. You can even order unusual shapes such as triangles, to fit one area (like a gable-end peak) and establish a unique feature.

Generally, new builds include the same type of window throughout. You may mix in a fixed "picture" window, but using one type establishes a uniform, pleasing look. Here are the basic types.

» **Fixed.** Just as it sounds, this is a window that doesn't open. These are used in barndos to take advantage of stunning views. They can be hard to clean but generally cost less than operable windows.

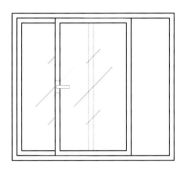

Double hung   Sliding sash

» **Double hung/Single hung.** In either version of this style, there is a top and bottom sash (both move in double-hung and only the bottom moves in a single). The look naturally suits a country-style barndominium. These are the easiest to maintain because the sashes either tilt in or are completely removable for cleaning.

» **Sliding sash.** This window has one fixed and one movable sash, which slides open and closed (bypass) horizontally in a channel. Sliding windows are a simple look well suited to most barndominiums. They are often less expensive than other types.

» **Casement.** Opened by a crank, the sash pivots outward along one side. Barndos rarely use casement windows. An open casement window interferes with passage along a patio.

Fixed

Casement

- **Window construction.** New windows are rarely just a single pane of glass. Almost every new window is "double-paned"—two layers of glass sandwich an inert gas such as argon. The gas increases insulation value. Triple-paned versions are a more expensive upgrade. Frame material also affects energy efficiency, budget, aesthetics, durability, and longevity. Here are the options:

» **Vinyl.** The most common new-window material.

THE GOOD: The least expensive option, vinyl frames offer a traditional look compatible with many home styles. Vinyl is colored as it's formed, so scratches show less. It won't rot or fade, requires virtually no maintenance, and is durable. Hollow frame spaces ensure excellent energy efficiency. Budget vinyl windows last between 10 and 20 years; quality units will be in good shape after 30 years. Premium vinyl windows carry a lifetime guarantee.

THE BAD: Vinyl windows don't take paint or stain, so the installed color is for life. Manufacturers offer a limited palette of colors (most vinyl windows are white). A vinyl frame is bulkier than other types; the glass surface area is smaller in a vinyl frame. Vinyl can also deform, and seals may fail, a common occurrence that leads to interior pane fogging, when exposed to extreme temperature variations over time.

» **Fiberglass.** Considered an upgrade from vinyl.

THE GOOD: Fiberglass is paintable, stronger, and more durable than vinyl. These frames can last 50 years or more. The material can be textured to look like wood and is 10 to 15 percent more energy efficient than vinyl. Like vinyl, fiberglass is maintenance-free. It will not deform, crack, warp or peel and is excellent for resisting high winds and severe weather like hail.

THE BAD: Fiberglass is 15 to 25 percent more expensive than vinyl and will degrade under long-term exposure to strong, direct sun (the surface will become unattractively "chalky.") But you can buy protective coatings. Fiberglass windows are also not as widely available as vinyl units are.

» **Aluminum.** A distinctive look that complements steel building components.

THE GOOD: Aluminum frames are incredibly strong; the natural strength means the frames can be thinner, allowing for a larger glass area. The look is a favorite with architects, and is a good option for a window wall of fixed windows. Modern aluminum windows can be ordered with thermal breaks to increase the aluminum's poor insulation value. The best aluminum windows last upwards of 50 years; inexpensive versions have a maximum life of 25 to 30 years.

THE BAD: Aluminum's kryptonite is moisture, especially in coastal saltwater regions. If you live where moisture is a near constant, spend more for a factory-applied anti-corrosive coating. Aluminum is also difficult to repaint and is a thermal conductor with poor insulation value. The material can fade over time and with direct sun exposure.

» **Wood.** The beauty and warmth make this a unique frame option.

THE GOOD: Expands and contracts less than metal frames do. The natural insulation value of wood is higher than any other window frame material. The look is unrivaled; staining or finishing can highlight the wood grain, and wood is easy to paint. It is durable and, if properly maintained, wood windows can and have lasted a century.

THE BAD: The most expensive window-frame material, wood requires the most maintenance. Wood windows are prone to warping, and susceptible to both moisture and insect infiltration.

» **Composite.** Following in the footsteps of composite decking, composite window frames are the newest addition to the field. They are extruded and can consequently mimic the look of metal or wood.

THE GOOD: Composite frames come in many looks. They are easy to paint, durable, and competitively priced, right between vinyl and wood. The color permeates the material, so scratches don't show. They can be recycled.

THE BAD: Composite frames tend not to hold up to hail and high winds as well as other choices do. They are also subject to the long-term wear like what vinyl may show.

Picture windows (or fixed windows) can be custom made to suit odd sizes and even unusual shapes, like the units here that follow the peak of this entryway roof.

Although costly, some manufacturers offer hybrids: wood-framed windows clad in vinyl or aluminum on the exterior. These windows offer the insulation value, durability, and appealing interior appearance of wood on the inside, with an exterior that needs less maintenance and can be more resistant to moisture and insects.

Manufacturers and suppliers will make recommendations based on your barndo. Builders and contractors have their preferences too. They will offer practical advice based on experience. Regardless, proper installation is essential, especially the exterior flashing and insulating frame purloin cavities.

If you're ordering your own windows, understand that window companies make windows to order, so it can take months to get a full set of windows built and delivered. Ideally, windows are installed right after the initial shell is built, so that they can be properly insulated with the rest of the shell. You don't want window delivery to hold up the whole process.

Installing your own windows is generally a bad idea, even for a skilled home craftsperson. The process is exacting, and mistakes become apparent only after the build has been completed, meaning they will be incredibly disruptive and expensive to fix. A skilled and experienced window installer or builder can adapt to situations and head off problems before they occur.

- **Skylights.** Some barndo owners install a drop ceiling to create an attic for storage. Most, though, make use of the roof's natural slope and create soaring vaulted ceilings. That opens up skylight possibilities.

However, skylights are problematic for metal-roofed barndominiums. Roof panel seams make skylights a challenge to install. Installing a single unit can run hundreds if not thousands of dollars. And that's not counting the cost of the skylight.

Skylights increase sunlight penetration, but potentially heat up the interior. The trick is to choose the right skylight for your barndo and location. Here are the options:

As impactful as a wall of windows might be, a more modest and still handsome row of south-facing windows allows a good amount of sunshine with limited solar heat gain, when shaded by substantial overhangs. That will translate to energy bill savings over the long run.

» **Plastic vs. glass.** Less expensive than glass units, these are usually tinted. They can be formed into many shapes, from flat to barrel shaped. They are about half the weight of glass, so they are easier to install and cause less structural strain. Double-insulated versions sandwich a layer of air and lower the U-value. Plastic is easily scratched, and often fogs or discolors over time.

» **Pricier glass skylights offer greater energy efficiency.** Today's units include thermal glass panes for safety; they shatter into many small pieces rather than deadly shards. Most glass skylights are double-paned. You can add a bronze tint for better sun reflection, a special Low-E coating, and argon gas.

» **Fixed or operable.** Fixed skylights are less expensive than any that open and close. But an operable skylight aids ventilation. These work with an extension pole or, with more expensive units, a remote-operated motor.

Decide on skylights before construction begins. The size and position will be included in plans to ensure skylights are correctly supported. Heavy units may require bridge bracing between trusses. That's done during frame assembly.

Tubular skylights are great alternatives. A roof lens hole usually fits neatly in a bay between seams, and the light is routed down along ductwork through attic space and a drop ceiling. Tubular skylights are installed after framing. They are a unique and inexpensive way to bring natural light into darker areas.

Understanding R-Value, U-Value, and Low-E

Once upon a time not so long ago, insulation values were easy to figure out. Insulation, doors, and windows all came with R-values. R-value is a measure of how well any physical barrier reduces transference of heat from one side to the other. Simple? Yes, but not for long, because science seeks complexity, especially when measuring things.

Enter U-value (sometimes called U-factor). U-value measures heat loss in relation to the difference between internal and external temperatures. Oversimplified, it's a more nuanced measure meant for materials such as glass, wood, or steel. U-value is relevant with windows or doors; R-value remains the definitive measure of insulation in walls, ceilings, and floors.

R-value can be improved by adding layers of insulation, which is why it's an imperfect measure of window and door insulation value. U-value is a better indicator of energy efficiency in those building elements. The lower the U-value the better: the best windows are .1, the worst are 1.

If that isn't complicated enough, throw into the mix "Low-E" glass. A low-emissivity coating is a thin, invisible metallic layer applied to glass. The coating reflects or absorbs sunlight UV rays, boosting energy efficiency. Low-E windows can cost up to 15 percent more but can boost energy efficiency by 30 to 50 percent.

R-Value

R-value is affected by two factors: density and depth. Here are average R-values for different types of insulation and building elements:

TYPE	R-VALUE PER INCH (2.5 CM)
Fiberglass fill (loose)	2.2–2.9
Fiberglass batts	2.9–3.8
Cellulose fill (loose)	3.1–3.8
Wool fill (loose)	2.2–3.3
Wool batts	3.3–4.2
Cotton batt	3–3.7
Cementitious foam (spray)	2–3.9
Polyicynene foam (spray)	3.6–4.3
Phenolic foam (spray)	4.4–8.2
Polyisocyanurate foam (spray)	5.6–8
Polyurethane foam (spray)	5.6–8
Window and glass door	2 (per unit; argon-filled double pane)
Door	5–6 (per door; fiberglass or steel-clad)

- **Cupolas.** Cupolas are decorative, hollow box frames mounted on barndominium ridges to dress up roof lines. Most simply fasten to the roof. Sometimes they supply ventilation or light through a roof opening. Cupolas can have peaked roofs, round domes, faux windows, louvers, and more. They can be built of metal, wood, or vinyl colored to match or contrast the building. A weathervane can top your cupola, adding authenticity.

Some suppliers offer prefab cupolas. You can also buy them from architectural ornament retailers or resellers, or even have them custom made. Although usually installed during initial construction, cupolas can be retrofitted.

Cupola Sizing

The general rule for sizing cupolas is 1¼ to 1½ inches of height, to 1 foot of unbroken ridge line.

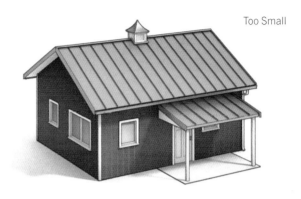

Too Small

Typical

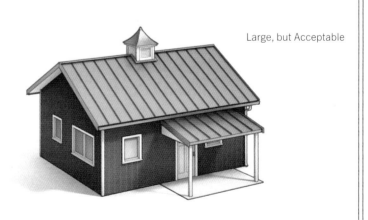

Large, but Acceptable

Cupolas can contrast or match the barndo. With a bold color like this fire-engine-red steel barndominium, it's best to match rather than risk a jarring visual.

Why add one cupola when you can have two? Here, two different cupolas tie together the sections of an L shape barndo, sprucing up an otherwise understated building.

- **Exterior doors.** Exterior doors play a bigger role in a new barndominium than they do in most homes. Barndo shells are well insulated and become energy-efficient "thermal envelopes." Exterior doors are potential points of weakness. That's why the most important choice is the largest—the traditional oversized gable-end door.

Barndominiums traditionally feature one or a set of oversized doors, although smaller barndo kits may not include these. This is not only an aesthetic feature, but also handy for moving large furniture and appliances into the newly constructed home, or driving vehicles into a garage.

Any exterior door should complement the barndo's style, provide adequate security, and meet budget. Even within those restrictions, there are many options:

» **Barn doors.** Sliding barn doors look classic. Although they hearken back to working farms, they are now considered a high-end distinctively stylish barndo feature. They are more expensive than sliding steel or roll-up doors and are typically crafted of wood. The doors must be engineered to slide in special channels so they don't become thermal weak points. That is why they are sometimes paired with hinged doors hidden behind the barn doors. They are better suited to timber frame structures than to metal barndominiums,

Roll-up, or swing-up garage doors involve a more complex opening mechanism and additional expense, but are usually more convenient and a good choice if one end of the barndominium will be used as a garage.

although given the vast range of styles offered, it's easy to find one to complement even a metal structure (see box Barn Door Styles, page 172).

» **Garage doors.** Many steel post-frame barndominium kits include a steel, insulated roll-up door. These are extremely practical, especially for a barndo that includes interior workshop or garage space, because roll-up doors are usually automated. Garage doors range from plain to units with windows and relief panels.

Most modern garage doors are well insulated. If you're building a barndo with a ridge peak 18 feet (5.5 m) or higher, buy an automatic door opener. That can be a significant expense, one that should be included in the total build budget. Less often, barndos are outfitted with steel garage doors that slide open and closed.

» **Gable-end options.** Some barndominium owners fill the gable-end walls with French doors or a wall of windows, or both. Those are especially effective to take advantage of a spectacular view or increase sunlight penetration. Where money is no object and a functional entertaining area sits right outside, you can even order accordion-style glass doors to fold out of the way. In any case it will be a trade-off. A wall of windows or glassed-in opening will have a much lower insulation value than solid doors or a wall would.

Hinged barn doors are a classic look, but need to be carefully installed to ensure that insulation value for the structure is maintained.

Entry doors combine a high-use feature with a design focal point. Spending a little more for eye-catching units, such as the French doors that dress up this barndo, is an investment few barndo owners regret.

» **Entryway doors.** Your barndominium's front door is the perfect place to make a style statement. Choose a wood-grained or wood door with a window for country appeal. Go with a simple linear modern or contemporary door to complement the style and lines of the average steel barndominium. Match the door to the siding if you've chosen a particularly striking wall panel. Or just stick with the front door supplied by the manufacturer, often a basic solid slab designed to blend with the building.

The entryway design will influence your choice. A well defined entryway, with an awning, overhang, or peaked roof begs for a more decorative door. However, if you choose an aftermarket front door, match measurements carefully. Barndominium doorways are structurally complex openings. It's very hard to change the dimensions once the building is fabricated. It's better if the door can be modified to rectify any discrepancies between jamb and opening.

» **Access doors.** Other access doors are typically left plain in keeping with the style of a steel building or a pole barn. Timber-frame barndos more often use access doors that mimic the material and style of the front door, or glass doors that complement the character of the wood structure.

Oversized, handcrafted traditional wood barn doors or a modern garage door wearing a disguise? Only the builder and homeowner know for sure.

Gable-end window walls (even a half-wall like this one) are some of the most stunning features a barndo owner can include in the building. Keep in mind, though, that this will significantly increase the budget and can lower insulation value of the shell.

The rust red of this barndo not only blends well with the natural surroundings, it is also distinctive and perfectly paired with a brown roof.

- **Exterior color scheme.** Steel barndominiums are painted during fabrication. The paint bonds so securely to the steel that you can often get 25- to 40-year paint warranties. Timber-frame barndos will differ if you're not using metal roofing or siding. Other materials may need to be carefully prepped, primed, and finished before exterior wood members are stained or sealed. In any case, repainting such a large building is no small task. You'll likely be living with your color choices for a long time.

  Barndo designers, builders, and owners go in one of two directions with exterior color: a scheme that blends in, or distinctive combinations that make the home stand out. Earth tones or neutrals are natural choices where the surrounding landscape is visually arresting. Tans, browns, or dusty green work well with wooded backgrounds or even high chaparral. Neutral beiges and off whites suit just about any location but lack excitement.

Owners increasingly choose vibrant color schemes to make the building pop and accentuate an unusual structure. Fire engine red-and-white is a traditional barn color scheme, and still a showstopper. Rich blue and yellow, or charcoal gray and orange can also be "wow" color schemes.

For all the beauty the right shade may offer, there is a practical side to color choices. If local winters are mild and the summers are long and hot, a lighter color scheme will keep the interior cooler over time. In a northern or western region, one at high altitude, a darker color will keep the barndo comfortably warm during snowy winter days and chilly spring and fall evenings.

- **Outdoor areas.** The last thing to design for an exterior is an outdoor sitting area. This can be as simple as a patio with roof, or an extension of indoor space. For instance, you might plan a covered porch off a great room, which would leave you the option to screen it in later. Where the climate is mild year-round, barndominium owners often design a full outdoor kitchen. This would also involve planning for electrical, plumbing, and gas.

Some barndo owners choose to use the savings from building their home to create stunning outdoor spaces, like this impressive kitchen.

Projection Protection

Commercial steel buildings often don't have gable or rake (eave) overhangs, or gutters. To minimize expense, roof edges terminate at the eave. That's an odd look for a residential barndominium and won't leave much protection for doors, windows, or sitting areas. That's why most owners plan for gutters and often include significant rake and eave overhangs, often with soffits, especially with any timber or wood-framed structure, which need to breathe.

Providing ample protection underneath from the elements, this metal roof overhang is significant enough to support soffits—the panels under the overhang that give it a polished, finished appearance.

Although the edge of a metal roof doesn't need to be finished, a fascia like the one on this modern desert barndo creates a wonderfully stylish look. The overhang includes metal soffits and integral gutters leading to the downspouts.

THE SITE PLAN

Before beginning an interior floor plan, most designers and pros draft a site plan, showing the exterior design. A proper site plan is a top-view 2D representation of how the new building will sit on the lot and includes details of the surrounding areas. A site plan normally includes:

- Positioning and size of physical landscaping elements

- Location of well if necessary

- Location of septic system, including leach field, if appropriate

- A key to cardinal directions

- Access road or driveway

- Nearby structures or relevant geological features

- Elevation drawings of the barndominium from end and side

The site plan gives everyone involved a clear idea of where the building will go, its orientation, and how it relates to landscaping and other property details. Correct measurements are crucial. Precision ensures the well company will not drill your water source where your garage was supposed to go.

There are three ways to create a site plan: use a professional, draw the plans by hand, or render them with a home design program.

The professional option involves hiring a site surveyor, who will take precise measurements, note sun direction, and even record average wind speed and direction. If you're already having the property surveyed, as may be required for financing, the surveyor will draft at least parts of the site plan. Depending on the property, a full survey and site map can easily run more than $1,000.

Your other option is to do it yourself. Many rural zoning authorities accept hand-drawn plans. However, you'll do better with something more precise. If you're comfortable learning a new computer program, you can create a plan with widely available home-design software. Most are user friendly. Some offer in-depth information based on GPS coordinates, which can

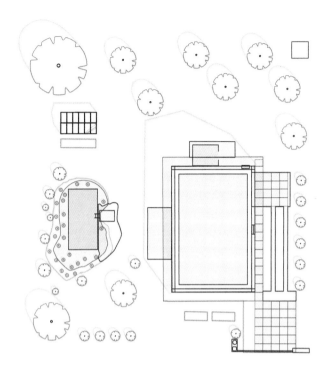

A detailed site plan like this can be the start of your own barndo dream. It's a road map to building success and takes guess work out of the process for the professionals involved.

reveal what to expect over the course of a year on the property. These programs often include libraries of features like trees and shrubs.

INTERIOR DESIGNS AND FLOOR PLANS

The interior floor plan is where a basic steel building becomes a home. It's a chance to more fully envision what barndo life will be like. Draft your own, have a professional draft a unique floor plan and elevations, or buy stock, existing floor plans for your barndominium's size and shape.

The floor plan is your opportunity to understand how people will move through the space and interact with each area. It gives you a window into how light will fill different areas. It's also a chance to make sure rooms are an adequate size and shape, and that using the home will be comfortable and practical.

Purchasing floor plans and blueprints is an easy way to leverage professional expertise. These are available for standard barndominium sizes, and many manufacturers offer plans with their models, and can even supply drafting services for custom projects.

A professional designer (see Case Study on pages 70–77) or architect can be a better choice for a totally custom barndo and is often worth the additional cost even if you're buying a prefab package. A professional with experience designing barndominiums can draft an interior floor plan at the same time as he or she creates the exterior plan, including truss locations, slab shape, and specifications.

The most important consideration as you plan from outside in is that the engineering elements are correct. That starts with a proper shell and appropriate, engineered slab foundation. Even if you've decided to create all the plans yourself, you would be foolish not to have the shell, roof structure, and slab engineered.

No matter who creates them, you will use the plans to solicit bids from builders and contractors. The more precise and complete they are, the better for the entire process and for accurate estimates. If you're drafting your own plans, here are the basic steps:

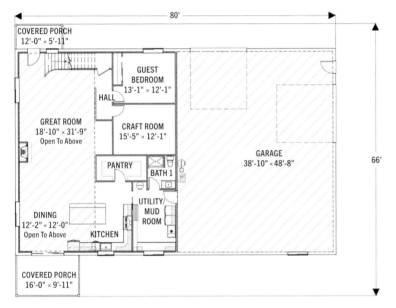

Example of a floor plan, including both the first and second floors. A plan like this offers a precise view of how the spaces inside the barndo relate to one another.

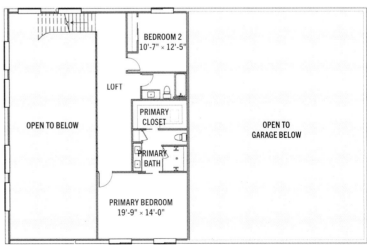

1. **Site plan.** Use the site plan footprint to trace the outline of the building for your first, rough floor plan sketches. This will provide the outline, inside of which you'll create your dream interior.

2. **Know local code and zoning restrictions.** Investigate code issues that might affect how you develop the interior layout. For instance, most local codes dictate where a hot water heater can be placed, and how much space is required around it.

3. **Consider site conditions.** Window placement and sun exposure determine what room goes where. For instance, if you will spend most of your time in a great room, locate that space so that it has the best views of any room. If you're a late sleeper, position your bedroom suite with a northern or western exposure, to limit early morning sunlight.

   Don't be too strict with yourself at this point. Don't hesitate to create multiple sketches of the interior. The more options you try out, the more likely you'll discover exactly where you want everything in the house.

4. **Budget.** A master suite with two-person jetted tub and overlarge walk-in shower may be the height of luxury, but you don't want it to break the bank. As you dream in pencil, edit with a more realistic eye on your finances.

5. **Finalize.** Initial sketches can be rough, but in refining floor plans as precursors to actual blueprints, make sure that:

   - Interior spaces and elements are to scale.

   - Doors and windows are clearly noted, including opening swing.

   - Locations of electrical outlets and fuse boxes are clear.

   - Surfaces, appliances, and other permanent fixtures are drawn to the proper shape and size, including air space around any appliance that requires ventilation.

Submittable Plans

At some point, you'll have to formalize floor plan sketches. They must be rendered as accurate blueprints for both builder reference and submission to local building departments. You'll need to turn to a professional or use a software package to produce professional-quality renderings. Even though in some rural locations and certain areas you may be able to secure building permits based on preliminary and hand-drawn plans, the best way to ensure success is to have precise blueprints for professionals on the project to follow.

Using a Design Pro

You can hand off the design duties to a professional designer (see Case Study on page 70), but given the unique nature of barndominiums, it's wise to find one with experience designing them. Some builders and manufacturers offer design services as well.

Finalizing Building Plans

Whether you've drafted your floor plans yourself, used a design program, or hired a professional, you'll ultimately need to print them out for submission to the building department, and distribution to contractors and subcontractors who will be turning the plan measurements into finished space.

Before you pay for final printouts, though, check with the local building department to verify its requirements for submission. What any building or zoning department requires varies widely. Financial institutions also have requirements about plans, so it's wise to check with your lender. Local building departments often put plan checklists on their website. A checklist will include the documents you'll need to submit for a building permit.

With your plans in hand, and dreams of your life inside your new barndominium bouncing around inside your head, it's time to get down to the work of building your new home.

CAD and Home-Design Software

Software companies inevitably market home-design applications on their ease of use. "Easy" is relative. If you're adept at learning new technology, mastering design software may not be a challenge. If, on the other hand, you struggle figuring out your new TV remote, using one of these programs could be more of an uphill climb.

Where once this type of powerful digital program (known as computer-aided design [CAD] software) was expensive and used only by architectural firms, now novices can buy affordable programs. Prices are far more reasonable than even a decade ago. In many cases, the software is sold through subscription. Here are the most desirable software features for designing your ideal barndominium:

- **Free trial.** This will let you get to know the program before going to the expense of subscribing or buying outright.

- **Furniture and appliance library.** The better the program, the more extensive the library of furnishings and appliance styles. Adding these elements gives you a more realistic idea of what moving around the space will be like. Playing with furniture position can lead to adjustments in room size.

- **3D modeling.** Most programs offer the potential to create both 2D floor plans and blueprints, and 3D models. Some programs even enable you to create a video for a walk-through tour of your unbuilt barndo.

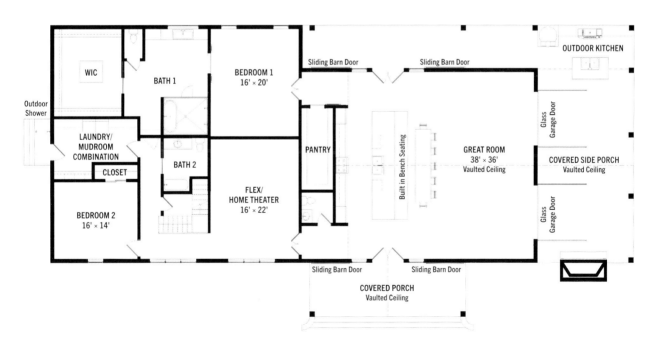

Hire a pro and get professional results. This floor plan was designed and executed by barndominium designer Stacee Lynn and provides a detailed view of how the spaces relate to one another and the exterior of the building.

3

Building a Barndominium Shell

Planning may seem like a hefty first step, but the longer and often rockier stretch is the building process itself. That starts with deciding who will build the home. Although you've likely already made that decision, there's no harm in revisiting your choice. You've probably discovered a lot through your planning and preparation.

Many factors influence the decision. Start with the financing. Any loan or financing package likely comes with strings attached. For instance, new-home construction financing typically prohibits owner builds.

Your decision also hinges in part on the type of barndominium. A builder, a general contractor, or the homeowner willing to act as contractor can reasonably build a barndo from a metal bolt-up kit. The same is true of a simple, rectangular pole barn. A timber frame structure, on the other hand, is best left to the highly skilled craftsman builder.

Custom barndominiums are a different case. Depending on the complexity, it's wise to hire a pro who has built unique barndos and is well versed in dealing with the construction challenges they present.

A tremendous upside to using pros, contractors, or builders is that if they make a mistake, they own it and fix it. If you make a mistake, you may be stuck. Beyond the choice of DIY or pro, you'll have to choose between a builder and a general contractor. The distinctions between the two can be a little murky, and the roles differ company to company and state to state.

USING A BUILDER

A home builder is a turnkey solution. Builders are often involved right from the planning stage. Some even offer custom design and planning services. If you're ordering a prefab kit, the manufacturer may recommend a local builder with whom they've worked before.

Builders know building and especially the buildings they construct repeatedly. A builder will have more significant in-house assets than a contractor would. Any builder you choose should be focused on constructing residential barndominiums, as opposed to commercial structures, or general renovation work.

The builder will control the process from site preparation through final walk-through. That includes setting build schedules, securing permits and arranging for inspections, and subcontracting out specific tasks for which the builder doesn't have onboard staff, usually electrical and plumbing.

The advantage of using a builder is that he or she is likely well versed in the challenges and problems that can occur constructing barndominiums in the local area. A builder is usually well acquainted with barndos, whereas a general contractor might not be as familiar. The builder may suggest changes he thinks will improve the home and will often cost slightly less than a general contractor. Lastly, for large, complex custom barndominiums, a full-service builder will likely be the clear best choice.

- **Using a general contractor.** A general contractor is a symphony conductor. Although he may not be able to tackle a given job himself, he will know how every part of the construction puzzle fits with all the other parts. Contractors have extensive professional networks and can quickly react to problems and even late-breaking challenges. A contractor also matches what he feels is the ideal trade professional to the project. This means the contractor has more flexibility than a builder.

  The primary value in a general contractor is efficiency. They generally work a little faster than a builder would, but still understand how to navigate permits and inspections.

  Contractors are often a jack-of-all-trades and may not have the deep experience with barndominiums that a builder would. They also don't come in until the work begins, which means they won't consult on the planning phase.

  If you're okay with being involved in the process as it unfolds, and like to keep tabs on anyone you hire, a general contractor may be the right professional for you. You serve as backup, ensuring everything, especially the schedule, is moving in the right direction.

Timber framing is some of the most beautiful barndominium construction, but requires a master craftsperson's touch.

The Pro "Must Have" Checklist

Different pros use different processes and methods. But legitimate experts follow best standards and practices, and are ethical, professional businesspeople. Any pro should:

☑ **Have experience.** Pros should have a track record of success with years if not decades in business. They should also have tackled barndominium projects.

☑ **Be licensed, bonded, and insured.** A lack of any of these is a deal-breaker.

☑ **Have references.** Get at least three, who hired the pro for projects like yours. Contact them and discuss their experiences.

☑ **Have a clean sheet.** Check with the local Better Business Bureau branch, sites like Angi, and similar resources to discover any red flags. Those include a current lawsuit filed by a former client or business associate, previous bankruptcy, and restarting the business under a new name.

☑ **Have won awards and certificates.** It's always a good sign when the industry recognizes a pro for excellence.

☑ **Show a businesslike demeanor.** This is more subjective than other issues, but no less important. How do they conduct themselves? Do they show up on time? Do they return calls or emails promptly? Do you get everything in writing, including the initial bid? These are all indications of how they will run your project.

- **You as contractor.** The DIY general contractor option is not for most people. However, if you have the energy and knowledge, and are willing to problem solve and learn as you go, you can save as much as 30 percent on the cost of a builder. This option is most realistic with kit barndominiums. A custom design, hybrid, or wood-frame structure usually entails too many variables for the nonprofessional. Regardless, areas of concern include:

  » **Punch list.** This is a simple checklist of tasks that need to be completed. It is a new-build contractor's best friend. Each construction stage gets written in chronological order. For instance, under "foundation" will be smaller tasks such as, "site level and graded," "stakes set," and "concrete supplier scheduled." No task is too small to go on the list. A barndominium punch list typically runs many pages. Although it can be paper or digital, it is consulted and updated every day.

No matter what role you're playing, it's essential to have necessary heavy equipment at the job site. This is critical for the heavy framing members and to perform tasks such as offloading delivered barndo kit components from a truck.

» **Schedule.** Scheduling is a challenge even for seasoned construction pros. Not only is it important to know timing specifics (e.g., how long foundation concrete needs to set before post brackets are fastened), you need to build in time buffers to accommodate unforeseen circumstances. An electronic calendar with automatic alerts on a phone is incredibly useful because it can be carried on the job site.

» **File system.** As helpful as apps and software are, any large construction project produces abundant paperwork. Critical documents must be organized and kept secure. These include subcontractor contracts, invoices and receipts, permit applications and permissions, and loan files. A project binder or accordion file serves the purpose quite well.

» **Contact list.** Anybody connected to or working on the barndo should be in a phone contact file. Any point person must have instant contact with the pros involved in the build. It's also essential to check on scheduled deliveries.

Choosing your builder or contractor is perhaps the most important decision you'll make. Being your own contractor is the riskiest option, but potentially significantly cheaper. Before deciding, honestly assess if you have the time and energy, and if you're willing to learn quickly as you go and patiently respond to unexpected situations.

With the point person in place, construction begins. A barndominium build looks chaotic at times, but it is a logical, sequential process. Each stage is completed in order, to ensure the least expensive, most efficient, and entirely successful build. The following are the general stages, although some builds involve others, or a different order:

Barndo Construction Overview

1. Site clearing and preparation (may include well drilling)

2. Foundation engineering and pouring

3. Shell construction, including post, pole, or stud setting, exterior framing as needed, and exterior roofing

4. Wall cladding installed

5. Windows and temporary doors (except in the case of barn or garage doors)

6. Exterior wall insulation blown-in or installed

7. Electrical and plumbing (some of this may be done on exterior walls, prior to insulation)

8. Interior framing

9. HVAC installation (some of this may be completed after finish work)

10. Flooring (usually staining and polishing the concrete surface)

11. Exterior pads for patios, driveways, and outdoor seating areas (may be done earlier with expansion joints between slab and pads, especially if there is a roof over the area)

12. Interior drywall hung

13. Interior finish work and final door installation (if temporary doors have been used)

14. Septic installed (this is done late in the process because heavy equipment and vehicles driving over a leach field can ruin it)

15. Landscaping and finish work

16. Walk through and inspection, final cleanup, and approval

The local building department can be an invaluable resource; many offer home building checklists to ensure code compliance and that inspections will fit the build timetable.

PREPARING THE SITE

Before actual building begins, the build site must be prepared. This ensures access for equipment and materials, and guarantees a successful foundation pour for the foundation. It's also a chance to remedy such problems as severe drop-offs in grade. Construction pros prefer a flat, level site not only for the foundation, but for areas on all sides.

Building dimensions are typically staked when the property is surveyed. Decisions about what trees, if any, to remove are made at that time and trees are marked with spray paint. The trees are removed, and the site is leveled and graded, and the soil compacted.

At or before this point, the access road and driveway may be leveled and graveled, allowing for construction vehicle access. Asphalt surfaces and concrete driveways are usually poured after construction, so that their relationship to the finished building can be adjusted if needed.

Wells are dug at this point unless the home will be serviced by municipal water and sewer. Municipal water supply and sewer connection involves digging trenches, running lines to the build site, and backfilling the trenches. Because vehicles driving over the leach field can easily damage septic systems, a septic system is installed after construction.

Site preparation is crucial for any barndominium, but some sites are more challenging than others. A sloped property like this one presents particular issues. The site had to be precisely graded, and only trees in the way of construction were removed, to maintain the look and feel of living in an evergreen forest rather than a clearcut hillside.

THE PERFECT FOUNDATION

A structurally deficient foundation is a life and death issue. That's why there's no excuse for not laying an engineered slab foundation, one that is properly reinforced for the weight and wind load of the structure, and the underlying soil type.

Engineering a post-frame barndominium foundation requires familiarity with the local soil conditions, understanding frost line depth, and a deep knowledge of torsional forces. Only an expert foundation company should engineer and lay your foundation. Although in rare cases a barndominium may be built on a basement or crawl space foundation, the vast majority are built on a stem wall or monolithic foundation. (The floating slab description is included here for information purposes.)

Barndominium foundations are typically built to match the width of the building, and 2 inches (5 cm) longer than the length. The minimum thickness of a foundation slab is 4 inches (10 cm), using 2,500 psi concrete. More commonly, monolithic, or stem-wall foundations are poured 6 to 8 inches (15–20 cm) deep, using 4,000 psi concrete. Deeper is usually better, but also more expensive. Engineered foundations are reinforced with a minimum of #3 rebar spaced at most 24 inches (.6 m) on center in a crisscross grid.

Correct placement and use of rebar throughout a foundation is the best protection against potential failure.

Examples of foundation types:

- **Floating slab.** Called *floating* because it's not fixed in place, this foundation is poured into forms set into prepared soil. This is the easiest and least expensive option. It is also the least stable and strong. Rebar is set in a grid, on bolsters, to reinforce against cracking under torsional forces. Laid in one pour, floating slabs are typically 6 to 8 inches (15–20 cm) deep. The deeper the slab, the more expensive it is, but the more it stands up to failure or undue shifting. Floating slabs are rarely used for barndominiums, and then only to support small buildings over extremely stable, strong soils.

- **Monolithic.** This term means that the perimeter footings and slab are poured at the same time. Footings anchor the slab from moving, protecting against soil shifting, compression, and other forces. Footings are poured deeper than the slab itself (usually 12 inches [30 cm] or more) and look like upside down T's in cutaway. This is the most common barndominium foundation. It balances cost savings and strength. Engineering is key. Footings must extend a certain number of inches below frost line, per local code, and rebar needs to be used correctly in both slab and footings.

- **Stem wall.** A stem-wall foundation is the most complex and expensive type used for barndominiums, short of a partial or full basement foundation. Feet are poured at depth and then topped by a wall of either poured concrete or cinderblock. The slab is poured separately as a floating slab with expansion joints along stem walls. This is ideal where significant fill has been used to level a site, anywhere the soil is prone to expansion and contraction, and for larger barndominiums.

An advantage to stem wall foundations is that the walls can be high enough to allow for a crawl space to route services through. That leaves pipes and conduit exposed and easily accessible for future repairs. Most, however, are poured flush with the top of the slab.

Most barndominium foundations require that plumbing be positioned when the forms are built, and the pipes are then encased in the foundation. If those lines ever fail or leak, they will require a complicated and expensive fix. But in practice modern plumbing materials ensure that this virtually never happens over the normal course of a barndo's lifespan.

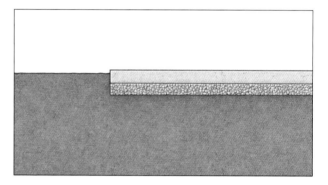

Floating slab

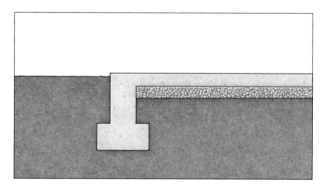

Monolithic

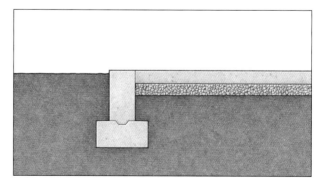

Stem wall

Pole Barn Foundations: A Special Case

Pole barn home foundations differ from standard types. The supporting posts are set in place before a reinforced slab is poured. The goal is to limit contact between laminated pressure-treated wood and the soil. The least expensive options are the most likely to fail in the short term. There are several ways the "poles" are secured:

A. Perma columns. Strong and durable poured concrete columns centered under each post. A "wet set" metal post bracket with rebar legs is set into the column right after the column is poured. Once the concrete sets, the posts are bolted into the brackets, creating an incredibly secure base. Posts are held above the soil line, so rot is rarely a problem. This requires professional expertise, making it the most expensive option.

B. Concrete post. A version of the perma column sometimes used in certain soil conditions or to accommodate specific loads. A concrete post, slightly larger than the wood post, is set into a concrete base. The post extends a foot (.30 m) or more above soil level, and the wood post is secured atop the concrete post in a steel bracket bolted to both posts. This is an expensive, long-lasting option.

C. Post sleeve. A high-density polyethylene (HDPE) sleeve is slid onto the end of each wood post. The post is positioned on the concrete pad. A partial backfill of crushed gravel is topped with soil. The sleeve extends a few inches above the soil line, protecting the wood. The sleeve material never degrades, so this support can last a century. It's easier and less expensive than a perma column.

D. Post-in-concrete. An older technique combining structural durability with easy installation. The post is set in place on a concrete pad. The post is braced plumb, and the hole filled with concrete. Wood expansion and contraction will cause eventual infiltration of moisture, dirt, and bacteria between wood and concrete. That leads to rot or post compromise. This shouldn't be used for pole barn homes.

E. Post-in-hole. The original installation method for pole barns. Simplest and least durable. The post is placed plumb on a concrete pad or tamped layer of crushed gravel, braced, and backfilled with dirt. Dirt-to-wood contact guarantees rot over time. Should not be used for barndominiums.

Once posts are set, the reinforced slab is poured. This typically entails compacting the dirt before the post holes are dug, and topping with a layer of compacted crushed gravel. A skirt board is attached between posts. Crisscrossed rebar is placed on bolsters in the slab field and the slab is poured.

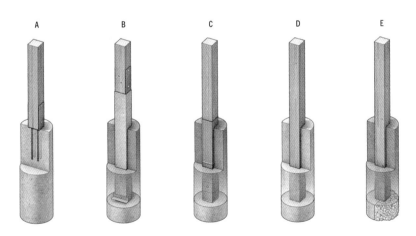

A B C D E

CONSTRUCTING THE SHELL

Once the foundation has cured, the supporting structure for your barndo shell can be erected. This is the skeleton for the rest of the home and must be built to exacting specifications to avoid future problems or issues with interior framing.

The overview that follows is how the process typically unfolds. Different barndominiums are built in different ways. If you're contracting your own barndo, follow the instructions that came with the prefab materials.

Covering all potential variables and methods of construction would take more than a single book, but the information here provides a guide of what to monitor as a builder or contractor works.

There are several ways to frame barndominium shells. These include all-steel skeletons, hybrid framing, and traditional timber framing. A smaller number of barndominiums are wood framed with wood trusses. Essentially, all involve sturdy supports along each side, bridged by trusses or rigid frame rafters. The roof structure connected with purlins and the walls with girts. Framing may include supporting components such as cable X ties to brace, distribute loads, and reinforce framing for individual openings. Here are a few examples:

- **Steel frames.** A barndominium kit normally includes all steel framing components. Here's a brief overview of how the steel skeleton will go together:

  » **Posts (columns) placed.** Beefy steel columns (the "posts" in post frames) are bolted to the foundation at specific intervals. Some builders lay metal welding plates in the concrete and then weld the columns in place. Heftier columns are sometimes used, so that they can be moved to accommodate custom window or door openings. Corner columns are often different from side or end posts because they must bear forces from both directions at once.

  » **Trusses or rafters.** The roof structure distributes loads from side to side, alleviating the need for load-bearing interior walls. Some barndos are built with simple rafters welded or bolted to the posts. Others incorporate webbed trusses. The type used depends on building size and style, as well as the manufacturer. Complete rafter-and-post units can be fabricated at the factory for ease of construction. But they are harder to transport, and more difficult to raise.

  » **Ridge beams, purlin, and girts.** Horizontal members connect and stabilize rafters or trusses. These are called purlins. Girts serve the same purpose across posts on the side walls. Ridge beams link trusses or rafters along the ridge. All of these make the building structure more rigid, as well as providing nailing surfaces for roof and wall panels.

  » **Openings.** Window and door openings, including metal jambs and headers, are fastened, or more commonly welded, into place to the posts, once the frame is up.

- **Hybrid framing.** Sometimes, especially with custom barndominiums, one or more walls may be stick framed. High-end barndominium designs may have a gable end wall framed in aluminum to accommodate a wall of windows.

- **Wood pole barns.** Some pole barn kits are designed to be supported like steel barndominiums, but framed like a more traditional stick-frame home. The poles are set, and then wood roof trusses, usually prefabricated with steel joint plates, are set in place, and the roof is framed out with a ridge beam or beams, rafters, and fascia plates. Doors and windows are framed in with wood as they would be in a stick-frame structure.

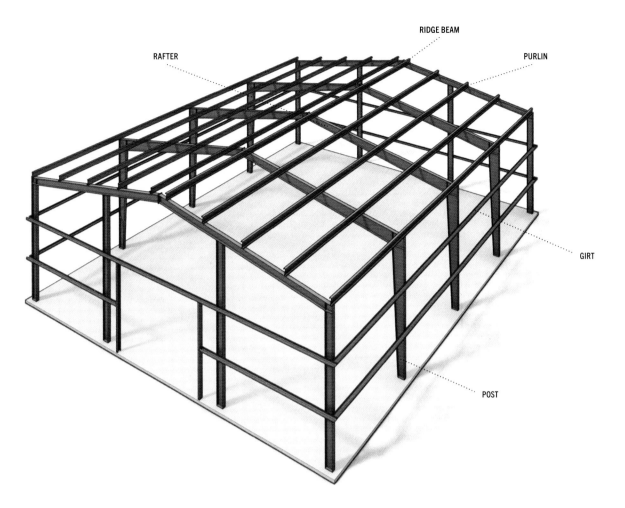

RIDGE BEAM

RAFTER

PURLIN

GIRT

POST

The basic structure of most barndominiums. In many cases, a full webbed truss will be used instead of single rafters. These basics are the same for timber or steel-framed barndominiums.

- **Timber-frame barndominiums.** Once the foundation is set, the timber is cut and staged on the site and construction proceeds rapidly. An experienced crew can raise a small timber frame home in as little as two days. Here is the method of construction:

» **Bents.** Posts for opposite sides are attached to a beam supported by corner braces, and to rafters meeting to form a ridge peak. The entire construction is called a "bent." The unit described here is the "common" bent, but there are different types. All bents needed for the barndo are assembled at the same time, on site.

» **Raising.** The bents are raised and the posts on each side bolted into foundation brackets.

» **Roof structure.** A ridge beam and top plates are installed, running the length, and connecting all bents. Additional rafters are added between top plates and rafter beam, and purlins may be added to reinforce the roof.

» **Walls.** Girts are often added across the posts to strengthen the structure. Windows and doors are framed out.

ROOFING

The kind of roof your barndo gets depends on several factors, from the material used to build the skeleton, to the roofing supplied with a kit. Installing metal roofing correctly requires exacting math and detail orientation. The stakes are high; an improperly installed roof can leak and cause thousands of dollars in damage.

Wood-frame pole barns, timber-frame barndos, and any barndo built of wood require roof sheathing panels as a base for roofing. Those panels are fastened to trusses or purlins, and covered with roofing felt, before the roof can be installed, unless you're using SIP panels, see box (at right). Steel barndominium roofs and walls are typically not sheathed; metal roofing is fastened directly to purlins.

A completed wood-framed roof. Notice the prefab trusses, and the underside of the roof sheathing on which the final roof will be placed.

What is an SIP?

Stick-frame houses have traditionally been clad in roof and wall panels, which are covered by building wrap and roofing felt to form a relatively air- and moisture-tight envelope. Steel prefab barndominiums' metal wall and roofing panels are attached right to framing members. The installation process creates the same tight energy envelope. However, hybrid, timber, or wood-frame barndos or pole barns normally require cladding like stick-frame houses, even if they are using metal wall and roof panels.

Innovative structural insulated panels (SIPs), are easier to install than other types of cladding, and offer superior R-value. The panels are screwed to framing members and the seams covered with special tape sold with the panels. Wood, timber, or hybrid barndominium builders usually clad roof and walls in SIP panels.

The surface of a traditionally seamed roof. The panels are fastened together with a seaming machine that creates thin, rolled spines from ridge to eave.

Many roofers opt for the easier option of a snap-together seamed roof. Each panel is snapped along the length of the seam to the panel before it. The look is slightly different, with squared-off ribs instead of the thinner spines.

Although timber-frame barndominiums can be covered with metal roofs, many are built with a traditional asphalt shingle roof. The vast majority of barndominiums are topped with steel roofing panels. These are fastened directly to metal trusses, purlins, or rafters. Here's the basic process of installation:

» **Measure.** Panel placement is measured and marked. End panels should be the same width to create the most pleasing look. Eave and ridge lengths are measured, and discrepancies noted. Panels are cut to accommodate.

» **Prep panels.** Panels are cut as necessary. Each panel is "hemmed"—the eave end is cut and bent under to create a U-shaped hem that hooks onto an eave cleat. Pros cut and close the exposed channel end for a more polished look.

» **Install panels.** Metal roof panels install quickly. A panel is screwed in place and each subsequent panel is then installed. Snap-lock seams are snapped securely together over their length. Seamed panels are seamed at the end of the process.

» **Install ridge cap.** Different types of caps require different installation methods. The method depends on whether the cap is for a vented or unvented ridge. In either case, brackets are attached along roof panel ridge ends. Ridge cap sections are fastened to these brackets, so that the cap overlaps the panel ends. Each subsequent section is screwed to the brackets and the previous section.

» **Flash hip caps and valleys.** Roofs with hips or valleys, such as wraparound patio roofs, require angle cuts. Those are made by hand to precise measurements. Hip caps or valley flashing are installed following the manufacturer's instructions for the type of roof. Properly fabricating hips and valleys requires skill and exacting placement.

Suppliers provide instructions for proper roof and wall panel calculations. They also provide fasteners, brackets, and other necessary hardware. The builder or contractor provides the tin snips, seamers, bending jigs, crimpers, and other installation tools.

- **Gutters.** Some metal roofs are designed without gutters and downspouts. The metal roof panels on a steep-pitch roof simply drain water over the eave.

  Where gutters aren't used, an overhang of at least two inches (5 cm) should be created on both eave and rake edges. However, many residential barndominiums are intentionally designed with deep overhangs that include soffits. Most are also fitted with gutters right after the roof is installed. Downspouts are installed after exterior wall cladding. Gutters are installed along eave edges with a slope toward the downspout of no less than $\frac{1}{8}$ inch per foot.

- **Cupolas.** Cupolas are installed after the roof is finished, because they are usually decorative (see Cupola Sizing, page 98). If the cupolas were included with a prefab kit, the installer follows the manufacturer's installation instructions. Install custom-made cupolas according to the fabricator's instructions.

Gutters for Good

Although some barndominiums are built without gutters because rain will naturally drip off a pitched metal roof, there are good reasons why you should include them. They certainly add to the look of the building and limit drips, but they can also be a way to collect valuable rainwater in areas that may be experiencing drought or water shortages.

Collected rainwater is considered a type of "graywater"—water that is reused in the home. Rainwater reuse systems range from the modest to much more expensive plumbed-in systems. The easiest is a barrel or barrels at the bottom end of roof gutters. However, if you plan ahead, you can integrate a sophisticated graywater system monitored electronically and recycling water not only from the roof, but sources like kitchen and laundry sinks, and showers.

In all cases, the water is not reused for consumption. Instead, it can be used to wash clothes, water a garden or landscape plants.

A pair of cupolas serves as the perfect accent to an understated single-level barndominium. They provide big visual bang for the buck that belies their inexpensive cost and ease of installation.

WINDOWS AND DOORS

Windows and doors are usually installed prior to metal wall panels on a steel frame. Timber or other wood-framed barndominiums are clad with wall panels before the windows and doors are installed.

Different builders and contractors use different processes. Some proceed through interior framing and the running of services before they install the windows and doors, to avoid breakage and make it easier to access the framing.

It's wise to use temporary doors and handles in place of final doors, until the interior is completed. Otherwise, workers might damage expensive doors while moving materials and equipment in and out of the building.

Measurements are crucial for door and window openings. A slight variation in frame construction can mean a prehung door unit (one already in its own jamb) or window may not fit as planned. That can involve returning the unit and ordering another, a time-consuming process.

It's not a good idea for the owner to install the windows and doors. Professionals have abundant experience working with the quirks of barndos and will ensure windows and doors open and close properly. Proper, expert flashing heads off leaks and drafts.

WALLS

Wood-framed walls were traditionally sheathed with oriented-strand board or other type of plywood. Barndo builders today usually use structural insulated panels (SIPs—see What is an SIP? on page 122) if they are sheathing the walls. SIPs are prefabricated, highly effective moisture and air barriers. They also provide significant insulation on their own, even before other insulation is added on the interior. SIPs install quickly and are sealed with special tape specifically meant for use with the panels. The panels provide a seamless thermal break that stops heat transfer through studs. SIPs also eliminate the need for building wrap.

Metal wall panels are then fastened to the sheathing. However, a wood-frame pole barn, timber frame structure, or other wood-frame barndo exterior walls can be finished with a different surface, such as traditional clapboard or wood shingles. Most barndominiums are covered in metal wall panels because the panels are easy to install, durable, and match the distinctive "barndominium" look and style.

In the case of a steel-frame barndominium, wall panels are typically attached directly to the posts or girts. The interior of exterior walls is then framed out in wood to allow for deeper insulation cavities and easy drywall installation.

Metal wall panels are trickier to install than metal roof panels. The panels can be run horizontally or vertically, depending on which look appeals to you, and which is more common for the type of panel you're using. For instance, batten-and-board style panels are typically run vertically, while "flush" panels are often installed horizontally.

Walls require even more exacting measurements and planning than roof panels do. It's essential to adjust panels around window and door openings, to create a balanced appearance and allow for the proper installation of flashing and trim. Corner wall channels require their own attention.

A basic "wood panel" pattern of metal wall panels is a traditional and handsome understated look. It has been spruced up somewhat here, with the use of a two-tone design. The look is embellished with the addition of white cupolas.

The installation process varies depending on the type of panel. Suppliers provide all necessary components and fasteners along with detailed instructions. Here is a simplified overview:

- **Layout.** Measurements and panel layout are crucial to a weathertight surface that looks as attractive as possible.

- **Starter pieces.** For most hidden fastener wall panels, the first pieces installed are inside corners, base trim, Z trim, and J channels. These often involve complex cuts to fit inside and outside corners; fastener requirements vary from supplier to supplier and among panel types.

- **Panel installation.** Usually, this involves screwing through a female flange. Subsequent panels are slid onto the previous or fastened with clips. End panels are trimmed with tin snips and fastened the same way into Z trim.

- **Window and door trim.** This is often the most precise part of an installation. Metal trim around wall openings not only creates a finished look, but it also protects from water infiltration.

Gallery:
DISTINCTIVE DOORS

Although barn doors—inside and out—are the type most identified with barndominiums, there are many distinctive styles that will suitably complement different types of barndos.

RIGHT: Heighten the barn door look with focal-point handles and hinges. It's easy to make barn door hardware an afterthought because the door style itself is so distinctive. But stunning handles like these add pop to plain-colored doors and enrich the look. Handles and hinges are available in any metal finish, from bronze to copper, and a range of colors as well.

Integrate a distinctive sliding barn door for a pleasing appearance. This bedroom has been designed with the popular white-and-gray color scheme. The construction of the bathroom sliding barn door offers a wonderful visual reference to the structure, but painting it the same color as the room's main door ensures it fits right in rather than jarringly standing out.

Go large for a big style statement. The bold character of most barndominiums can easily support dynamic architectural elements, like these double-size sliding barn doors. In keeping with the modern need for insulation value, the doors conceal more conventional French doors and header-topping windows. Painting the doors in lighter, complementary colors to the siding draws attention to what is a standout exterior feature.

Opt for simple in a contemporary room. Although it's tempting to go with a traditional rail-board-stile construction when using an interior sliding barn door, a contemporary decorating scheme and design style is often better served with a seamless rail-and-stile frame with solid panels. Painted the clean white of the room trim, this door is lovely, understated accent to a subtle interior design.

Turn to sliding door hardware for a showcase visual. Although more expensive than a basic package of sliding door hardware, a version like this makes great use of the wall space, becoming as scintillating a visual as wall-mounted art. Of course, the function remains, so that extra cost is a two-for-one value.

Choose frosted glass for light and sophistication. A second-floor bathroom stuns with a gleaming wood floor, but the sliding door grabs attention as well. A sturdy wood frame holds chic frosted glass panels that allow for maximum light penetration throughout the space, but provide plenty of privacy for anyone using the bathroom.

INSULATION

Once the shell has been framed and enclosed, it's time to insulate. Often the builder first runs plumbing or wiring that needs to penetrate the shell. Interior walls are insulated to diminish noise and sometimes to isolate the room for zone cooling or heating. But that is done after the interior is fully framed out.

Most barndominium exterior surfaces are insulated with some type of spray foam. The most common type is polyurethane because it has the highest R-value. Other less expensive foams may be used in mild climates, or specific circumstances. Regardless of the polymer used, there are two main types of spray-foam insulation: closed-cell and open-cell.

- **Closed-cell.** This is comprised of tightly clustered bubbles, creating "closed cells." This is denser than open-cell, with a significantly higher R-value, but also a higher price. Closed-cell spray foam expands to 1 inch (2.5 cm) thick, making it ideal for shallow cavities. The look is also tidier than the appearance of open-cell insulation. Closed-cell is most often used to insulate ceilings, where the limited expansion and high insulating value are ideal.

- **Open-cell.** The significantly lower cost of open-cell insulation can translate to major savings when used for a large barndominium shell. The structure is

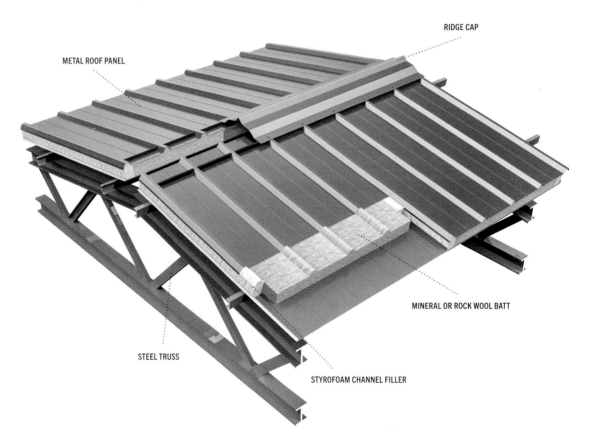

RIDGE CAP

METAL ROOF PANEL

MINERAL OR ROCK WOOL BATT

STEEL TRUSS

STYROFOAM CHANNEL FILLER

Although spraying foam insulation in the rafter bays is the most common way metal barndos are insulated, there are other methods. For homes in locales with severe winters, the homeowner can choose insulated roof panels constructed much like SIPs (see page 122). Instead of being fastened right to the trusses, the metal roof sheet sandwiches mineral wool or other high-efficiency batt insulation, with a sheet metal subroof used to fasten the panels to the trusses. Additional insulation can be added in the rafter bays to increase the R-value to exceptional levels.

made of bubbles that are incomplete, creating open cells. The spray foam expands to 3 inches (7.5 cm) and is more flexible and adaptable than closed cell. It is also a better sound dampener. That's why open-cell is most used in barndominium walls, where it will fill deep framed wall cavities and it expands even into small nooks, crevices, gaps, and odd-shaped openings—including the inside of window and door frame steel purlin cavities.

Wood-frame and timber-frame barndominiums are often insulated with closed-cell spray foam for the ceiling and fiberglass batting on the walls, like what is used in a stick frame home.

Spray-foam insulation is quick and simple and is often the ideal solution for the large area a barndominium shell represents. It is, however, far from the only option. Wood-framed structures, or any that are clad with SIPs or other wall cladding, are candidates for rolled or batt insulation. Although the batts or rolled insulation is usually fiberglass, for its combination of relatively high R-value and relatively low cost, Rockwool can be highly effective as well. Blown-in insulation is rarely used, except on interior ceiling joist cavities (see the next chapter for more on that).

With the shell and exterior squared away, the interior awaits. Since interior framing is more familiar to most people, an experienced DIY craftsperson will often jump in to frame out the living spaces.

Insulation Types		
MATERIAL	**FORMAT**	**APPLICATION**
Fiberglass	Batts, rolls, blankets, and blown-in loose fill	Easy to use, ideal for shallow standard wall and joist cavities
Rockwool	Batts, rolls, blankets, and blown-in loose fill	Easy to use, ideal for shallow standard wall and joist cavities; harder to work with but greater R-value than fiberglass
Plastic or natural fiber	Batts, rolls and blankets	Rarely used in barndos
Cellulose	Blown-in loose fill	Usually used only in hard-to-access areas and specific applications like attics; rarely used in barndos
Polyurethane	Board or spray foam	Board insulation only used in certain areas of barndo construction, including between skirt boards and slabs for pole barns; a common spray-foam polymer used for barndo ceilings and walls
Polyisocyanurate	Board or spray foam	Board insulation only used in certain areas of barndo construction, including between skirt boards and slabs for pole barns; a common spray foam polymer used for barndo ceilings and walls
Phenolic	Board or spray foam	Board insulation only used in certain areas of barndo construction, including between skirt boards and slabs for pole barns; a common spray foam polymer used for barndo ceilings and walls
Cementious	Spray foam	Less common spray foam used for barndo ceilings and walls
Polystyrene	Board	Board insulation only used in certain areas of barndo construction, including between skirt boards and slabs for pole barns

4 Creating an Interior

It's time for that floor plan that you fussed over so thoughtfully to come to life. With the shell and slab in place, there is now plenty of support for interior framing, systems, and finish work.

There are lots of reasons the barndo shell must be enclosed, and windows and doors installed, before beginning interior framing and finish work start. First, building the interior offers the opportunity to adjust to any changes in dimensions or openings that might have been made during exterior construction.

A weathertight shell also means that interior work areas will be cleaner and the environment more comfortable to work in. Lockable windows and doors, even temporary doors, secure the interior, protecting tools, equipment, and supplies left there overnight.

Some builders and contractors speed up the construction process by framing the interior before the outer shell is completely enclosed. This allows easier movement of wood framing materials in and out of the building, but it also exposes the wood frame to exterior elements such as hard rains. It's more common to frame the interior after the shell is complete.

FRAMING INTERIOR SPACES

All interior framing measurements are closely checked against the floor plan. There may be variations that the actual framing has to account for.

Certain adjustments will be made for the unique construction elements of a barndominium. For instance, although not every pro does this, it's wise to check the concrete surface under a sole plate for dips. The simplest way to do this is to run a chalk line at head height above the sole plate location. The pro levels it with a line level, and then, with the sole plate in position, measures down from the chalk line to the plate every foot of length. Variations can range as much as $\frac{1}{8}$ inch to $\frac{5}{8}$ inch (1–4 cm). Studs are then cut to different lengths, or shims are used under the sole plate.

- **Building basic interior walls.** Interior walls are usually framed lying down for convenience's sake, and then lifted into position. The builder or contractor will start with interior framing for exterior walls. These can be the most difficult, because they have to include framing around doors and windows, and have to tie in to other exterior walls at corners, and other interior walls at T connections. They also must be secured to the exterior steel frame if there is one.

Interior barndo framing looks like a house within a house. This is one of the unique facets of barndominiums and allows for adaptability and structural integrity.

An open floor plan with minimal wall framing maximizes available floor space and creates an appealing visual flow. You can define spaces with furniture or with fixtures such as the cabinets that mark the boundaries of the kitchen in this barndo.

Quick Check

Your builder or contractor can connect interior walls to the exterior metal frame of a metal barndo in a couple of ways. Many professionals fasten 2×4s to girts and nail the interior wood framing to them. There's a better way. Request that your pro use hurricane ties to connect interior framing members with exterior metal frame pieces. These secure the walls together but allow for normal building movement without damaging walls.

The walls are built of 2×4s, with sole plates (the bottom), studs every 16 inches (40.5 cm), and top plates that are doubled up to allow for properly securing the walls in the corners and at T connections with other inside walls. The walls allow for 8-foot (2.4 m) ceilings unless otherwise specified.

Doors and windows get specially crafted framing. Additional studs on the side of the opening support the opening, with a large "header" above it. This will create a deeper than normal window well, which is finished with drywall. There you can install a window seat where you can read or daydream away sunny afternoons.

Door openings are built out in much the same way as windows, although the sole plate is cut out over the threshold. Door jambs will be covered to make one oversized jamb.

Interior walls are framed on the floor and then lifted into position. This allows the walls to be moved around, so that builders or contractors can make last minute adjustments. Once the framing on exterior walls is in place, individual rooms can be framed out, including closets, water closets, water heater enclosures, HVAC (heating, ventilation and air-conditioning), closets, and pantries. Bathrooms and showers are framed in around preexisting drains placed before the slab pour.

Timber-frame barndominium interiors provide examples for how interior walls and structures relate to the exterior framing. Here, electrical conduit concealed in drywalled walls is exposed as it runs to ceiling fixtures because the framed roof is left exposed to show off the wood. Timber framing includes many unique features like this.

A loft like this is only possible through adequate framing between floors. Many barndo builders used 2×8s (5×20 cm) on top of first-floor walls, even if 2×6s (5×15 cm) are acceptable. The added depth allows for additional services and provides a uniform surface for a loft or storage area floor.

Quick Check

Most barndo owners opt for stained and sealed concrete floors. It's an easy way to have a beautiful, durable surface underfoot. Floors are finished after interior framing is completed to avoid damage to the floor appearance. This means the interior wall base 2×4 sole plates may be exposed to moisture during floor sealing. The sole plates may not fully dry out before drywall is installed. For that reason, it's smart to ask a builder or contractor to line the bottom of all interior sole plates with "seal" tape or other type of moisture seal barrier prior to when the walls go up. Also ask that framers use only blue chalk to snap lines; red chalk can stain the concrete.

Designed by a barndominium designer (see Case Study, page 70), this bathroom took more planning and construction than may be apparent. Plumbing for a freestanding tub such as the clawfoot unit here often requires routing a drain and supply where they normally wouldn't go. The best time to do that is before the slab is laid for a first-floor bathroom, and during framing for a second-floor room.

- **Second floor or attic.** Once all the walls have been placed and tied together at the corners, the layout should again be checked against the floor plan. This process requires care to to maintain nailing surfaces for drywall. This is one of the final moments when modest changes will have minimal impact.

  The builder, contractor, or framer will fasten 2×6 (5×15 cm) or 2×8 (5×20 cm) joists on the walls' top plates. Using 2×8s (5×20 cm) is always a good idea, but consult with your builder or contractor. The members not only provide a nailing surface for ceiling drywall, but they also form the second floor. If your plans don't include a second floor, this will likely become a loft or a storage area.

  The framers may also fasten 2×4 nailers across the undersides of steel roof purlins, running from walls to ridge, if the ceiling is to be finished.

- **Services.** Plumbing, electrical, and possibly HVAC are usually installed before interior walls are insulated. In many cases, this involves drilling holes in wood framing members, including studs and top plates, as well as installing electrical boxes, plumbing braces, and stub outs. Local building department inspectors will inspect these before the walls can be closed with drywall:

» **Electrical.** Wiring is run from the power main, through the breaker box, and on to individual outlets and fixture locations throughout the barndominium. This involves drilling holes through wall studs and sometimes top plates. Working with the framing wide open makes installing fixtures easier and quicker.

» **Plumbing.** Running pipes and installing drains and service fixtures gives you a chance to see specifics on where to place tubs, showers, and sinks. Attention to detail is essential because a leak can cause mold growth and rot inside walls.

» **HVAC.** New barndominium builds typically include a closet dedicated to the air handler for the system. Ductwork is routed from that location throughout the building to provide air conditioning and heating, as well as proper ventilation. HVAC ductwork is usually routed in joist cavities because there is no way to route them under the structure. In some instances, running ductwork may involve framing a "chase," or faux wall box. Explore alternative methods because chases are generally considered unattractive.

▪ **Insulation.** This is a last point before your interior takes on its final appearance. The builder or contractor (or DIY builder) will typically do interior insulation themselves; it's usually not a subcontracted task because it does not involve spray-in or blown-in insulation.

A few barndo builders exploit the additional wall cavities on the side walls that have been framed with wood, spraying in open-cell foam. This essentially doubles the layer of foam and insulation value on exterior walls, and overspray is easily cut flush with the inside edges of the studs.

But it's wiser not to do this. Some electrical wiring and potentially even plumbing will be run through the wood framing on exterior walls. Should you ever need to access those services for repair or remodeling, it's a major task to remove the sprayed-in insulation. That's why most builders either leave the wood-framed exterior wall cavities unfilled or use batts or roll insulation that can easily be removed if the need arises.

Although you don't need to insulate interior walls, most barndo builders do, as a sound dampening measure. The rare downside to the wide-open spaces and concrete floors of most barndominiums is that sound tends to bounce around and penetrate throughout the structure. That said, insulation can also help isolate a bedroom or other interior room if a zone HVAC system has been installed (in which you can turn off the heating or air-conditioning in other spaces and just use it in each room).

Because R-value is less of a concern on interior walls, most professionals use batts or rolled fiberglass insulation. This is inexpensive, easy to install, and effective at blocking sound. It is cut to fit around pipes and wiring, using a basic utility knife. It is installed in one of two ways: "Tabbed" batts (with the facing extended to create loose stapling surfaces on both sides) are stapled into wall cavities, which keep them in place before drywall is installed. However, unfaced roll insulation is a less-expensive option. Friction batts are simply stuffed in the wall bays, and friction holds them in place. These tend to bulge out on one side or another.

Is someone in the family a night owl while others go to bed early so as to rise early? This can make sound transmission a more important consideration. Spend a bit more and you can specify Rockwool for the interior insulation. Rockwool comes only in unfaced rolls and batts and is cut and friction fitted into the wall bays. Rockwool is not only a superior sound dampener, but also essentially fireproof, and repels moisture rather than absorbing and holding it.

No matter what kind of insulation you use, interior walls don't generally get vapor barriers. It also doesn't really matter which direction you install faced batts, unless you're insulating between an interior room and an unheated area such as a garage. In that case, the facing should be oriented to the heated side.

You'll be wise to inspect the interior wall insulation and back up your pros by using vapor barrier tape over any holes or tears in insulation facing.

- **Finish the floors.** Any wet process such as staining and sealing concrete or pouring epoxy is usually done before hanging drywall. Other types of flooring such as wood, laminate, or tile, are installed after the drywall. If the concrete floor has been properly poured and leveled, you have a wide range of flooring options from which to choose. Here are the most common:

» **Finished concrete.** Most new barndominium owners finish the concrete slab for a unique, visually stunning, and remarkably durable floor. Concrete can be stained in several shades; the most common is amber. The stain is sealed with a clear, protective epoxy top coat. After the concrete floor is sealed, it's protected with Kraft paper or drop cloths while the drywall is hung, and painting and finish work are completed.

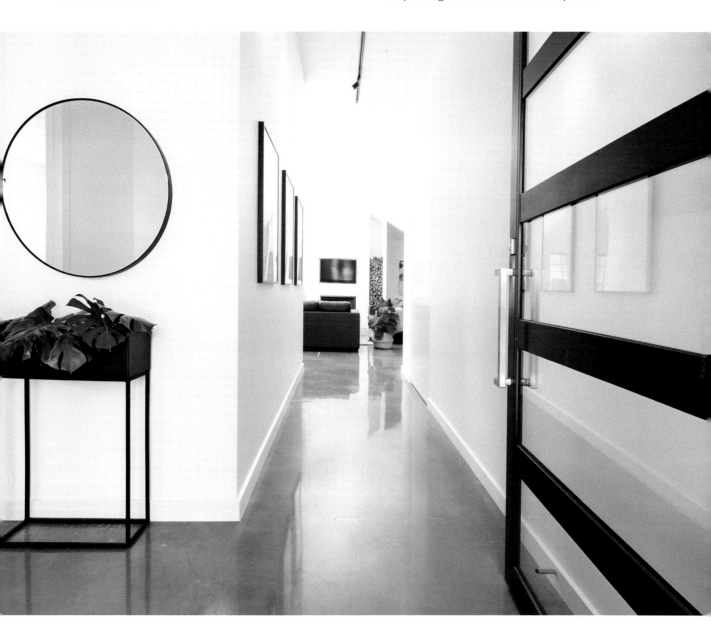

A properly sealed concrete floor, left natural in this home, is the literal and figurative stage for all the other decorative floor elements.

Concrete can be scribed and finished in a matte sealant to look just like tile. It's an interesting treatment that is not for every space but can be impressive.

» **Decorative epoxy.** Epoxy flooring got its start as a highly durable surface option for commercial and industrial builders. Early floor epoxies were limited to institutional blues and grays. These days, there are much more impressive decorative epoxy options. They include deep, rich colors and metallic epoxies that can look like swirling mist underfoot.

You can also choose one of the many "flake" epoxies that look just like the name sounds, with embedded colored plastic flakes. The concrete floor is prepared as it would be for staining and sealing, with the epoxy mixed, poured, and carefully spread over the floor. Epoxy floors are incredibly durable and won't fade, discolor, or stain. But they can be tricky to apply and get just right.

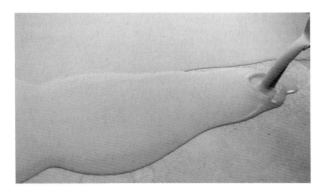

Modern epoxies are pourable self-leveling formulations, but require meticulous preparation of the concrete underneath.

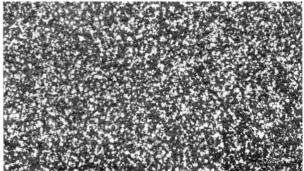

Just one of the many hues available in epoxy flake coatings. These can make for a fascinating look and also hide dirt and grease in workshops and garages.

» **Tile.** A clean, level concrete surface is a great base for stone, ceramic, or even glass tile. Given the large square footage of most barndominiums and the high cost of tile relative to other flooring, most barndo owners limit its use to kitchens or bathrooms. Even in a small area, the right tile can have a huge visual impact. The wide variety of surface appearances and designs means that there is a tile out there for any preference and interior style.

» **Laminate.** Inexpensive, easy to install, and fairly durable, laminate flooring is great for common areas of a large barndominium, or the entire floor area of a smaller structure. "Click" plank or strip products are installed over a pad, as a floating floor, not fastened to a subfloor. Laminates are manufactured with a photo-realistic layer under a clear protective coating, convincingly mimicking other options, such as a wood flooring, ceramic tiles, and even abstract patterns.

» **Carpet.** Carpet is rarely used on barndominium ground floors because it is not a natural complement to the look. It's also difficult to install because the perimeter tack strips must be fastened to the concrete surface using masonry fasteners. A common exception is in upstairs bedrooms. Second floors are framed and built with plywood subflooring that you can easily cover with carpet for comfort underfoot.

» **Wood flooring.** Wood floors are almost never used in a barndo because they require laying a wood subfloor first, then nailing the flooring to it. Laying a wood floor over concrete is expensive and labor-intensive. The exception is the second floor of a tall barndominium. Because the plywood subfloor is part of any second-floor framing, the base exists to lay a wood floor.

A properly engineered and laid slab is an excellent base for laying tile, like this large-format ceramic version.

Laminate strip or plank flooring can easily and quickly be installed right over concrete. A foam underlayment is used to provide additional cushion. The installation is basic enough for even a novice DIYer.

Gallery: FLOORING

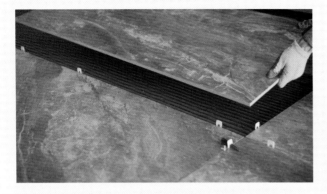

A well-laid slab foundation provides an ideal base for stunning, large-format stone tiles. The tiles can be pricey, but they are a great DIY floor project in a kitchen or bath, and they create a uniquely beautiful, super durable, cleanable, and luxurious surface underfoot.

Plain wood can be distinctive. Although a natural finish is fine, if you're covering your concrete barndominium floor with wood, consider more scintillating alternatives. A dark stain and matte finish like the one in this stunning living room creates a dynamic stage for the rest of the interior design.

LEFT AND ABOVE: Less expensive than wood or most tiles, linoleum turns the hard surface of a barndominium's slab into a warm and cushy treat for your feet. It doesn't stain, and it's waterproof, so clean up is a breeze. Last but not least, the incredible range of looks available ensures that there's a linoleum product to suit any barndo owner's tastes.

ABOVE AND RIGHT: Laminate floors are a less-expensive option to real wood or stone tile surfaces. The material convincingly mimics the look of many different wood species and types of tile from ceramic to marble. Best of all, laying a laminate floor is an easy DIY project even for the novice. You can purchase thresholds to create borders between a laminate floor and the concrete surface. This allows you to limit the floor to, for instance, a bedroom or office.

Vinyl sheet or tile floors are inexpensive, cleanable, long-lasting and come in a vast range of appearances. Vinyl flooring is a good choice in areas such as kitchens and bathrooms, where moisture is a constant and a little cushion underfoot goes a long way.

Where concrete would have been cold and fought the other elements, the wood floor fits right in with the reclaimed quarter-sawn wood wall, timber fireplace mantel, and windmill ceiling fan.

Gallery: KITCHENS

A kitchen often serves as the social center of a home, but no more so than in a barnominium. The barndo kitchen is much more than a place to prepare meals and is often integrated into an open floor plan, so that the border between great room and kitchen is blurred. Here are specific issues to keep in mind when designing your barndo kitchen.

1. **Function.** Even though barndo kitchens are typically larger than average home kitchens, that's no reason to ignore the need for a "work triangle"—an efficient relationship between prep surface, refrigerator, and cooktop. Before any other consideration, the kitchen has to be easy and pleasant to use. Each leg of the triangle should be as short and direct as possible, and should equal the length of the other legs as much as is reasonable.

2. **Center the action.** Determine where the center point of the kitchen will be. This will often drive traffic flow in and around a barndo kitchen. For instance, many barndo owners focus food prep and social interaction on oversized islands placed in the middle of their kitchens.

3. **Keep views in mind.** In most cases, the barndo kitchen will look out to more than one adjacent space, and possibly out through an end wall out to the surrounding landscape. When positioning seating areas and work areas, it's wise to consider how views will impact anyone using the space.

Exploit island space for multiple functions. Although it's a wonderful food prep surface, a solid surface island like this should do double duty in a barndominium. Given the large square footage of most barndos, homeowners typically add a large farmhouse or dining room table. That means a large kitchen island is the most common way to add an informal eating area to the kitchen itself.

Gray goes well with barndos. It might not be the first color you'd think of, but a simple gray for your barndominium kitchen is exceptionally compatible with the country nature of the architecture and—frequently—the location. As a bonus, gray cabinets show less dirt than white does.

Use style indicators to establish your kitchen design. The type of sink you add can set a tone for the whole kitchen. Here, a distinctive apron-front farmhouse sink with a gooseneck faucet screams "country kitchen," and perfectly complements the barndominium's natural vibe.

Exploit a view, even in the kitchen. Although it would have been easy enough (and less expensive) to use this gable end wall for additional kitchen storage, the homeowner opted for a stunning window wall with glass doors. That choice creates show-stopping views for anyone eating or preparing meals in the space, and created a link to an outside deck and dining area. The exposure also boosts natural light penetration—a plus in any kitchen.

Create visual drama with contrast. The black wall color in this barndo kitchen offers a dynamic visual variation on the traditional all-white, subdued kitchen design. Notice that the color is used sparingly, because it could easily overwhelm the room. With a little restraint, the color is perfect relief to the more sedate decorative elements.

Layer lighting for a clean, efficient barndo kitchen. The mix of natural and artificial light in a high-ceilinged barndominium can do funny things to the light at different times throughout the day and night. It's always wise to ensure work surfaces and the entire kitchen are well lit, something achieved in this room with a mix of undercabinet, overhead, and accent lights.

- **Wall surfaces.** Hanging drywall is not technically challenging, but it can be much more difficult in a barndominium than in a traditional house. How complex this process is depends on whether the ceilings will be finished with drywall and left vaulted and on how many interior walls have been built.

  Although some DIY-minded potential barndominium owners hang their own drywall, it is quicker to leave it to the pros. Because of the large wall expanses, builders use 4×12' (1.2×3.6 m) sheets rather than the more common and manageable 4×8 (1.2×2.4 m). It takes experience to work deftly with the larger sheets.

  Cement board is installed in bathrooms and other areas with significant moisture exposure. At the same time as they install wall surfaces, the pros will enclose the interior areas of windows and doors.

- **Trim and molding.** Trim and moldings are the jewelry on your wall surfaces. Some barndo owners prefer the clean, modern look of doors, windows, and walls with no trim, but you should at least consider baseboard moldings to cover any irregular gaps at the bottom of walls.

  You can buy vast numbers of molding profiles, from simple boards to more curvy and ornate shaped moldings. Pick a look that complements your intended interior design. The more basic the style, the easier it will be to install. You'll also choose between extruded polyurethane moldings and wood types. Polyurethane moldings are flexible and paintable, and easy to work with. But wood is the professional's choice if the molding will be stained.

Quick Check

Does sound bouncing off the shell in your new barndominium bother you? Ask your builder or contractor to use "quiet rock" (special sound-dampening drywall) when they install wall surfaces for bedrooms or other areas where quiet will be king.

A timber-framed barndominium like this is so visually busy that any window or casement trim or molding would be excessive.

- **Specialty ceilings.** Vaulted ceilings offer a lot of dramatic design potential. Although you can simply drywall your vaulted ceilings, there are other options worth considering.

A wood ceiling with boards run gable end to gable end can be painted, stained, or sealed for a natural look. You can choose wood for its unique grain pattern or use a combination of woods for an eclectic look. Get back to the barn roots of this home style by cladding the ceiling in reclaimed wood boards that bear the marks and patina of age. Wood ceilings are a natural for timber-framed or wood-framed pole barns and barndominiums. But they look just as stunning in a steel barndominium, and they help suppress noise.

Want a unique look? How about a pressed tin ceiling? You'll find a wonderful array of reproduction looks from online suppliers, and a tin ceiling is not much more difficult to install than a wood board ceiling. But both will cost you more in materials and labor than a drywalled ceiling.

Tin is only one metal that can adorn vaulted ceilings. A country interior will be well served by a corrugated metal panel ceiling. Up the authentic vibe by using reclaimed rust-streaked panels. The panels will be much easier to install than other types of ceiling cladding, and they won't experience exposure to the elements, so they are unlikely to deteriorate any more than they already have. That's not say, however, you can't use brand new bare metal or painted metal panels. Follow your instincts to determine the surface that will best service your overall interior style.

Cladding a vaulted barndo ceiling—especially in a timber-framed home—allows distinctive features like the trusses here to draw the most attention. Drywalling the ceiling also allows for placement of recessed lighting, both a functional and aesthetic addition.

Wood-paneled ceilings are a natural choice for any type of barndominium. Here, the ceilings are complemented by a country windmill-style fan, and a circular staircase that matches the steel trusses.

Once you finish the flooring, walls, and ceiling, the dimensions and specific spaces of your new home will reveal themselves, with a mother lode of design potential. Now it's time for the most enjoyable part of the whole process: finishing your interior and outdoor areas.

Quick Check

Before finalizing purchase and delivery of appliances, double check all measurements to ensure your chosen refrigerator, stove, washer, and dryer fit into the space as built.

5

Finishing Touches

Choosing and adding interior design elements is the way you put your own signature on a new barndominium. It is how you turn a simple barn-inspired structure into a "home." Let your creativity loose, your imagination run wild, and the ideas flow. You can always edit out options that are too much or too expensive. This chapter will guide you through a logical process of finding and expressing your creative voice.

Keep in mind that this is an intensely personal process, and it should be a pleasant one as well. Indulge your creative method. Whether that means physically sketching out ideas, or walking around your newly completed interior space, dreaming of what could be. The only wrong interior design for a new barndo owner is the one with no thought put into it.

You might be thinking, "Why is this the last chapter, and not the first?" Good question.

Enlightened interior design considers the characteristics of the building and its surroundings. The journey from blueprint to newly built barndo inevitably leads to some surprises. You won't really understand the nature of the interior space until you have a chance to move around in it. The same goes for exterior elements, like the view through a large window or the amount of sun any room receives throughout the day. The great thing about designing after the build is that you're no longer dealing with what you imagine the space will be; you can respond to what it is.

This is where the right insulation pays off. A divider wall between a TV room and a bedroom ensures that a minimum of TV noise sifts into the bedroom. The sliding barn doors seal more completely than it appears, helping muffle noise transmission.

Contemporary room designs are accommodating of style elements from other distinctive styles. This living room includes a comfy contemporary couch that sets the mood of the room, but the exposed timbers identify the architectural style. The windmill fan is a country touch, while the brick fireplace surround is traditional.

Start the design process by defining your style. Homeowners often call their style "eclectic," but that may mean that they haven't really defined a style. Lack of a design style isn't really a style at all.

Even if you don't want to label your style, think about what defines your own aesthetic tastes. Do you like clean, crisp lines, minimal clutter, and centerpiece furnishings? Or do you prefer a cozier, more informal look and feel, with rooms full of overstuffed furniture and family memories? Maybe you're drawn to bold colors. Perhaps you're more of a muted, sophisticated grays-and-blues type. Developing your signature barndominium look means understanding those preferences and using them as guideposts.

Your look will likely be unique to your home. However, any barndo interior is usually inspired to one degree or another by the most common design styles in this type of home.

Checking the Details

Before you add finishing touches, make sure the construction is good and truly complete. Deal with any issues before the professionals pack up their tools and equipment and head off to the next job.

Here is a basic walk-through list of details to check before signing off on construction. (This is sometimes called a "blue tape" walk through, because it's common to mark problems with blue painter's tape):

- Turn on all lights to check that they work and have bulbs.

- Check all outlets for power. You can use a cell phone charger or cell phone.

- Open all doors including cabinets—and check vanity and cabinet drawers.

- Check the walls behind doors to make sure they were painted.

- Check inside closets to ensure all surfaces were painted.

- Turn on and operate all appliances.

- Ensure that the heating and air-conditioning work.

- Run the water in all faucets and showerheads.

- Flush toilets and check for leaks.

- Open and close all windows.

- Inspect the breaker box to see that the breakers are clearly marked.

- Check that there are no obvious gaps that need caulking around countertops and other bathroom and kitchen surfaces or fixtures.

DESIGN STYLES

Here are the styles that look most natural in a barndominium. This doesn't mean you have use any of them, but they can inspire ideas and hone in your focus.

- **Country.** Although there are many types of "country" interior design styles—French country, English cottage, horse country—the one typical of barns and barndominiums is Early American, or traditional country. This is the plain old "country" style of country music and the ranches and farms that characterize the American untamed West.

The style is comfortable, warm, welcoming, and informal. The look embodies the simple, slower nature of country living. Furniture is rustic and sturdy. The homes feature abundant use of wood and other natural materials for furnishings and trim, and such fixtures as cabinetry. A country look focuses on simplicity, practicality, and utility, and rarely includes more formal elements such as symmetrical furniture placement. Country interiors embrace imperfection, for example an aged wood beam with the scars of time, or a rough-hewn concrete countertop.

This contemporary kitchen creates a calm, clean feeling with neutral colors and uncluttered surfaces. The understated nature allows eye-catching details—like the subway tile backsplash and bistro style stools—to grab attention.

Rusted tin sheets for a ceiling surface, black accents, rough brick wall, and an old fashioned heating stove add to the industrial feel of this space. It's raw, bold, and eminently attractive.

- **Industrial.** Just as it sounds, this style has its roots in commercial and industrial buildings. Given that steel barndominium structures share those roots, the style is a natural match for a new steel barndo. An industrial look showcases unfinished raw building materials, such as iron, copper, concrete, brick, and steel. The focus is on pure function and the "guts" of the building are left exposed: framing, HVAC ductwork, and even some cast iron plumbing. Spaces are sparsely furnished with simple, rough-and-tumble furniture.

- **Modern.** Even though this style derives from working farm structures, the large interior spaces of most barndominiums lend themselves surprisingly well to a modern aesthetic. This style is defined by monochromatic color schemes, usually whites or neutrals, clean lines, minimal decorative elements, sophisticated use of art and pictures, and polished, reflective surfaces.

Modern interior style doesn't need to be cold. This simple and elegant modern great room is made welcoming with a white stone fireplace column, abundant textiles, and pillowy furnishings.

The look may include occasional bold color splashes, such as on an accent wall or a vanity front. Modern interiors are meant to be clean and spare, and have a crisp, new feel with no flaws. Lighting is bright, sparkling, blue and visually cold, as opposed to the warmer yellow incandescent lighting used in country style.

- **Contemporary.** This is a slippery style to pin down, because 1980s contemporary is not today's contemporary. However, certain style indicators define contemporary interiors at any point in time. Understatement is key. Colors are usually subtle, neutral and background. Such surfaces as counter-tops are polished and finished, but not with luxury materials. Rooms are light and airy, and furnishings are simple shapes and crisp lines. Subtlety is key, and shapes and forms are squared off rather than ornate. Upholstery and textiles are more often solid color than patterned.

THE MOOD BOARD

Okay, so you've thought through your design preferences and inspirations. Now it's time to get down to the nitty gritty—exploring actual design elements. Fortunately, there is a tried-and-true method for organizing inspirations, ideas, and focal points. It's called a mood board, and it's an invaluable tool interior designers far and wide use. It's a wonderful asset for homeowners as well.

A mood board is a collage of materials and inspirations collected on a large piece of cardboard, foam core, or even plywood. It can also be created digitally, using an organizer program or specific mood-board applications. Pinterest serves as a mood board for many people. But a physical mood board allows you to consider and appraise samples, from the purely visual of a color square, to the tactile allure of a small fabric sample, quickly and easily.

The goal is always to combine patterns, colors, textures, and looks against a white background to determine how well design elements work together. The mood board can be as precise or vague as you prefer. It almost always includes inspirational photos, textile samples, and color inspiration. But it can also include rough room sketches with keys to where things will go. Here are some of the basic elements you can put on your mood boards:

- Room, furniture photos, or other images from magazines, books, or online sources

- Photos you took from nature or interiors

- Sketches, as appropriate and necessary

- Fabric samples

- Other samples, such as countertop chips or metal pieces that you'd like to include

- Color chips or sample color squares painted directly onto the board

- Words that express your design theme

A sample mood board. Yours should include any kind of photographic or physical sample that might inspire your design.

Don't be too critical making your mood board. Collect a variety of appealing samples, colors, examples, and style ideas. Once you have a broad selection, you can edit down your choices to get to your final design elements.

Remove anything that clearly doesn't fit with the rest. Establish themes in color use, materials, shapes, and lighting that can be repeated throughout the interior to tie the design together. Identify cornerstone elements, such as an eye-catching sofa, overlarge piece of art, or exceptional lighting fixture, that will grab the most attention. Your style will evolve as you make these decisions.

Keep in mind that everything left on the board after you revise and edit is a design building block. From the fabric on a throw pillow, to the distressed finish on a wood country-style dining room table, everything needs to support the overall theme, and the look and feel of each given room.

Interior Design Tools

A pencil and a sketch book or just plain paper serve as a good starting point to craft the look of a room or your entire interior. Begin with sketches. They don't have to be polished and can include just enough detail to represent the room (top left) or use grid paper to create a more precise drawing (bottom) if that works better for you. Then consult your details and other samples until you find the combination of textures, color, and form that best complements your barndo and speaks to the look you're after.

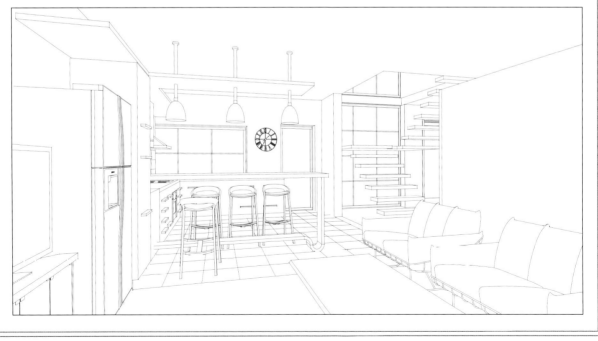

COLOR

Homeowners often make color decisions too late in the design process. The color scheme for your design will cover everything from throw pillows to small appliances, to what shade you paint the walls.

Because textures and natural materials usually dominate barndo interior designs, paint color is often less of a consideration. That said, it's still an important design consideration.

Most barndo owners lean toward white or neutral walls. The architecture usually speaks loudly for itself, and hallmark features like exposed trusses provide plenty of drama. Lighter colors or whites also accentuate wide open floor plans and the sheer interior size of many barndominiums. In lighter and nondescript colors, walls and ceilings become backdrops to impressive exterior views, other interior design elements, and interesting parts of the structure.

Barndo owners love gray, like the light tone used on these walls, because it allows other details to pop, like the black barn door sliding hardware.

That doesn't mean you have to use neutrals. Maybe you prefer bolder or more distinctive palettes. Although you probably don't want a dark or bold color on every wall, strong color can be wonderful in the right places and in small doses. Experiment with color in furniture, art, accents, and other elements that can be easily changed if the color doesn't work. You can tie the overall design together by using splashes of bold color throughout the space, on appliances and art, for instance. A visually interesting variation on wall color can turn doors into simple design elements.

Remember that darker colors and matte finishes absorb light, while lighter colors and glossier finishes reflect and amplify it. Here are color families to consider:

- **Gray.** A subtle step up from pure white or neutral colors, gray is sophisticated, understated, and contemporary. Darker grays are usually a little too dour for a barndominium, but a lighter shade can be an effective choice for an office or guest bedroom.

- **Black.** Yes, black. Certainly not the first choice of homeowners, black can be a powerful accent if used judiciously. Interior designers sometimes use it to "outline" spaces on the trim. Black is also extremely powerful coupled with certain other bold choices in small areas, such as paired with fire-engine red on a door.

- **Red and orange.** Use either of these sparingly. Red is a visually hot color that excites the eye and can increase your heart rate. Red and orange hues can be striking in small pops. They are also best used in rooms where you don't plan to relax.

    You would not find a red or orange bedroom very restful. Used too widely, either of these colors can overpower an interior.

- **Blues and greens.** These are both complements to barndominiums' natural surroundings. Green especially links the spaces inside to outside trees and shrubs. Blue links to the sky and water. Stronger greens can be ideal for kitchen or bathroom cabinet fronts.

Accent bold color for emphasis. Pairing colored walls with furniture and accents in complementary tones is a way to boost the visual power of both. This silver lamp pops against a strong blue background; a yellow or black accent would work just as powerfully.

Use special effects to make subtle colors sing. Neutrals like this stately gray are common among barndominium interiors, but neutral doesn't have to mean boring. The rag rolling technique used on this accent wall creates a stunning mottled appearance that draws the eye while maintaining the elegant nature of this color.

CREATING THE DESIGN: START BIG

Start with the largest elements and what you already own to "build" your interior design. That means placing furniture. Here are some basic rules to help you do that thoughtfully:

- **Choose a hero.** Place the "hero" piece first in any room, say the largest piece of furniture, or the most distinctive one you want to attract all eyes.

- **Consider traffic.** No matter where you put furniture, it cannot impede traffic flow. The arm's length rule is useful to place side and coffee tables. Any table should be reachable from the chair or couch closest to it.

- **Balance visual weight.** Furnishings and decorations carry visual weight according to their size and bulk. Don't cluster the heaviest, bulkiest pieces in one area or on one side of the room. The same is true of large, open-floor space areas versus crowded sections of the room crammed with furnishings. Visual weight should be balanced.

- **Create social zones.** Furniture placement should invite relaxation and interaction. The grouping around a coffee table for instance is a traditional socializing area. Larger rooms should be designed and laid out with more than one social zone. Thinking in terms of discreet zones of interaction is a way to work through a room's design (e.g., "I want the kids and their friends to watch TV over here; I'd like us to gather at holidays or family game night in that area.").

- **Experiment and adjust.** Keep in mind that interior design is a process of trying out different options. Don't be afraid to move around even large pieces and try out unconventional layouts.

- **Reflect.** Mirrors are actually furniture as well, though they may seem like art, accents, or afterthoughts. For such simple pieces, they have an oversized impact on interior designs. The right mirror in the right place will visually expand a room, making it airier and lighter. A mirror frame provides a decorative accent.

You don't have to do all your design in the physical space. You can play with furniture arrangement on a sketch ($\frac{1}{2}$ inch to 1 foot [1.5-30 cm]), or use an interior design program. Most programs have libraries of furniture and accents to represent what you already own, or to dream about what you might want to buy.

RIGHT: Barndo owners spend a lot of time in their kitchens, so consider how you'll move around the space. Here, the range and refrigerator form a perfect "work triangle" for easy and efficient food prep. Every room has traffic flow considerations like this. They're more important in a space with unmovable islands.

LIGHTING

Light fixtures are unique elements in your interior because they serve two roles: sources of illumination, and design accents. Start with function before considering form; a fixture that doesn't provide enough light is a design defect, no matter how beautiful the actual fixture. There are three basic types of home lighting, and they should be combined and layered in any room design:

- **Ambient.** This is the general lighting an overhead fixture provides. Ambient light fixtures should be the first fixtures you plan for. Ideally ambient light sources will be dimmable to accommodate different moods and situations. Dimmers are often already in place as part of construction, as they are with recessed lights.

- **Task.** Task lighting means just what it says: fixtures meant to make tasks easier and in some cases safer, for example reading lamps and under-cabinet fixtures. Task lighting also fills in shadows from light that ambient fixtures cast. Task-lighting fixtures should also be considered decorative accents and are the second layer in a lighting plan.

- **Accent.** Often called "highlighting," accent fixtures focus strong light on a particular object or area. Think of these fixtures as spotlights. The focus might be a work of art, the glassware in a cabinet, a fireplace, or other architectural feature. Accent lights are the third and final layer in a lighting plan and supplement the other two.

A beguiling mix of suspended fixtures, wall sconces, cabinet lighting, and lamps ensures excellent all-around illumination for the dining area, and draws attention to the many wood details in this timber-framed structure.

A multifaceted lighting scheme more than serves this bathroom. Note the side-mounted lights for the mirror; those are preferable to fixtures over the mirror because they create more accurate mirror images.

Many people don't give much thought to a "room lighting plan," but that's a mistake. The proper illumination shows off the best features of any room, makes the space easier to use, and ultimately even determines how welcoming an interior space will be.

Lighting behind a TV or behind where viewers sit is much more effective than a light that shines right on the screen. The same goes for windows. If a bright light fixture is pointed at a wall of windows, for instance, it will cause glare and reflections that will obscure the nighttime view through the window.

Create your own lighting plan. Supplement overhead ambient fixtures with wall sconces as needed. Ambient fixtures are the best place to start a lighting plan, because they usually can't be moved. Add task lighting around the space to accommodate functions you intend to do there. Task lighting can also be used to fill in disturbing areas of shadow anywhere ambient light doesn't reach. Finally, add accent lights to showcase artwork, structural features, or other attractive elements such as glassware.

Individual fixtures should match your design theme. Consult the mood board often to ensure all elements including lighting reinforce the central theme. Although designers define three types of interior lighting, fixtures can serve more than one role. For instance, a multi-head floor lamp may fulfill all three types of lighting.

DOORS

A barndominium is not a traditional type of home. One of the most obvious indicators of that reality is the over-large gable-end door (which is sometimes replaced with a wall of windows in custom structures) that is so often a hallmark of a barndo. Whether that is a traditional set of sliding or hinged barn doors, or a roll-up steel door, it's a nod to the historic barn and farm roots of this type of building. That's also why sliding barn doors are so often used in barndominium interiors. Sliding door hardware complements any interior barn door's distinctive style.

Barn doors are only one of many options. Since there are no load-bearing interior walls, you can size interior door openings as you wish, rather than conform to traditional stick-and-frame code standards. Outfit a primary bedroom with beautiful French doors or choose pocket doors. You can certainly use traditional panel or slab doors if those better capture your style.

Barn Door Styles

Barn doors are the height of simplicity: a few planks held together by rails (horizontal face boards) and stiles (vertical face boards). Cross braces can add a bit of style. Simple as they are, those basic elements offer a diversity of potential looks. For more options, you can leave the field and face boards natural, stain or paint them, or even color them with contrasting tones. The illustrations here are the most common patterns; you can design your own.

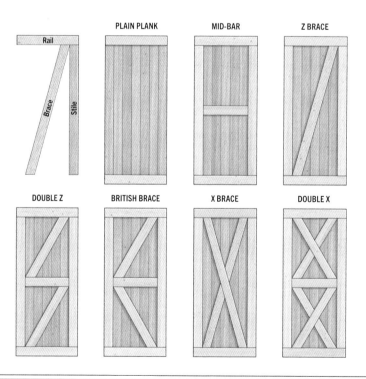

Interior French doors can add tons of style as they do to this doorway inside a custom-designed barndominium. They also let more light in.

ACCENT TO EMPHASIZE

By this point, your interior design has jumped off the mood board and become a livable, wonderful interior. Rooms focus on serving their purposes as attractively as possible. The furniture is placed, the spaces well lit, and individual room plans finalized. Now it's time to add the jewelry on your interior design: the accents.

Accents are the icing on the cake. This is your chance to personalize your barndominium and really claim it as your new home. The best part? Accents are easy to add and simple to edit, and most are changeable whenever the mood strikes you:

This ground floor living room comes to life with a distinctive windmill fan, unique wall decorations in the form of words, fun throw pillows, and other accents. They turn a simple room into a statement.

Accents tend to play particularly large in a barndo kitchen. The baby blue island and stools in this eclectic space brighten the space a bit, and create interesting visual tension with the simple pattern and color in the rug.

Hang your art thoughtfully, whether it's family photos or original prints. Think out the composition before you hang, not after. Play with the shapes. As a rule, it's best to keep the same spacing among all photos and align at least one edge with framed art next to it. Both of those rules are bent or broken here, but it's done carefully to maintain an eye-catching arrangement that does the photos proud.

▪ **Art.** Art is personal, but make sure you edit your art and photos. The wrong print or sculpture, even if you love it, can disrupt a thoughtful interior look. If you want to do your barndo interior design justice, you won't start by saying, "This picture has to be included." Instead, you'll go back to your mood board and start with the question, "Does this art fit with the theme as it has developed?"

Many new homeowners crowd all the blank spaces on walls with art or pictures. It's better to leave some blank space so there is more emphasis on particularly remarkable or personally meaningful art.

Before you hang anything, measure and sketch where the art will go and how to arrange different pieces. Or cut foam-core board or cardboard to the size of individual pieces of framed art. Then you can tape them in position and move them around until you have the most pleasing visual composition.

Eye-catching hexagonal tiles trade on the visual power of line and shape, rather than bold color. It's a good match for a modern barndo kitchen.

Who says drapes and curtains are only for the inside? Here, a bold barndominium designer has not only furnished and accented a covered outdoor patio, but she also added poetic flair with drapes hung between the steel framing elements. It's a unique and daring treatment that pays off big.

- **Tile.** Leverage the beauty and diversity of tile to spruce up your interior design. Add a kitchen or bath backsplash of hand-painted, glass or stone tile. Smaller tiles work better for smaller spaces. Mosaic tiles can make a backsplash a showstopping feature.

- **Window treatments.** Since key focus points of any new barndominium include the views around it and the isolated privacy of large property lots, most barndo owners do not use window treatments. But there is no rule that says you can't.

  Blinds are a natural addition to the look and feel of most barndominiums. Normally, the only time drapes might be used is in a bedroom to block light and for privacy. Light-blocking blinds can serve that purpose with far less impact on the interior design than drapes. But if you're a fan of drapes, they can add drama and texture to your interior design.

The Rule of Three

The symmetry of a pair of objects creates a formal, balanced appearance, but it is not as exciting to the eye as odd numbers. Hanging an odd number of framed prints or photos in a grouping with be more visually exciting than even numbers in a pairing or grid. The same goes for any sculptural decorations on shelves, mantels, tables, or even floors.

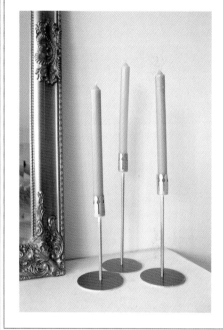

Gallery: BARNDOMINIUM-WORTHY TABLES

The right table can be as much a style statement as a high-use piece of furniture. You'll live with your dining room or kitchen table every day, so choose wisely.

Exploit the grain patterns of unique woods. Wood tables are the most common in barndominiums, but that doesn't mean they should be bland or boring. Choose a table made from an unusual species of wood, such as the maple surface here, and you'll be rewarded with a scintillating grain pattern and look that never grows old.

Isolate a dining room table to center the room. Whether you create a faux tile rectangle on a concrete floor, or use a rug on a wood floor as the barndo owner did here, the idea is the same: make a visual stage for the table. It's an attractive look and an effective design device to draw the eye toward the main piece of furniture in the space.

Consider Swedish style for a distinctive barndo appeal. Blonde wood and clean lines define the Nordic look that graces many Swedish farm houses. The same simple, handsome, alluring appearance can work to your barndominium's advantage and add a light, welcoming charm to your dining room.

Set a special stage for a simple table. The inlaid tile in this floor sets the dining room table apart from the traditional concrete surface. The tile contrasts the simple lines of the table, with the same durable, cleanable character. It's a way to dress up a high-traffic area.

Go with glass tops to preserve wood tables. Add sparkle and amplify available light by topping a wood dining room table with glass. It's a wonderful look when coupled with other eclectic elements, such as the wicker chairs in this dining room.

Match a wood table to metal accents. Basic wood tables are all well and fine, but you up the visual excitement when you pair a wood surface with metal framing elements. The black metal here—and a glass block base—really pops against the natural finish of the tabletop. The table becomes more than the sum of its parts.

AT HOME OUTSIDE

The large property lots on which most barndominiums are built lend themselves to outdoor living. In fact, many new owners specifically specify outdoor kitchens, or just covered patios, using those areas as actual extensions of the indoor space. Most people, though, limit themselves the far less expensive option of a simple wraparound patio extending the foundation slab, with an overhang roof attached to the main structure.

This allows for a spacious sitting area where homeowners can relax outside.

Building an outdoor relaxation area is not the only option. A flat, level, compacted area of ground outside the back door can accommodate a grill, table, and chairs. Take a step up and buy or install a firepit and create a conversation area where you can enjoy socializing and stargazing in equal measure.

A flagstone patio dressed up with potted plants and an umbrella-shaded table complement an outdoor sanctuary for the homeowner to indulge in natural surroundings. Left bare, that space would be pretty but wasted.

You can also complement your barndo with a more traditional flagstone patio, or one made of pavers. This gives you the option of adding to the area as time and budget permit. You might choose to include an outdoor fireplace, a hot tub, or even terrace a slope to create different outdoor areas. Large property lots lend themselves to a wealth of possibilities.

A modern barndo is well matched to an exterior that blends a variety of textured surfaces: river rocks, flagstones, and the compacted desert sand. A bubbling in-ground fountain is the perfect finishing touch.

EXTERIOR LIGHTING

Lighting is no less important outside your barndominium than it is inside. Exterior lighting ensures safety, especially in a location that may be exposed to significant wildlife. More than that, though, lighting is your chance to set a mood, and make the home welcoming at night.

As a rule, exterior barndominium lighting should extend to walkways, driveways, and exterior seating areas with foot traffic after dark. The best type of exterior fixtures are directional, shining a narrow beam of light downward. More ambient style fixtures can ruin the nighttime views from the home. Subtlety is key in exterior lighting.

BELOW: The exterior lights on this modern barndo are appropriately understated, illuminating just the patio sitting areas. No light spillover pollutes the yard or surroundings. Safety lights on the garage serve a more practical role.

The exterior lighting on this barndominium offers maximum drama and sophistication. The gable end fixtures not only wash the surface in delicate light, but they also serve as decorative features themselves. Uplights around the patio landscaping add drama and are a wonderful look for any barndominium.

THE CHANGEABLE HOME

Keep in mind that both the exterior and interior design of your barndominium are organic. They should evolve as you do. Tastes change, and so can art, and even outdoor sitting areas. When grandchildren are on the scene, perhaps you want to put a pre-fab play structure outside. Couples who become empty nesters might want to turn a former kid's bedroom into a home gym. Although the underlying theme will probably still drive the look, different pieces of puzzle will move, come in, and be taken out over time.

If you've made it this far, you've created an amazing barndominium life that is comfortable and rejuvenating, and a home that is beautiful inside and out. Consider one final step to make this home even more personal—name your barndo! This is a wonderful way to celebrate the unique character and lifestyle captured in your new home.

Choose a name that is both fun and meaningful. This makes your barndominium even more than a home: it becomes a member of your family and cherished gathering place.

No matter what name you give it, you'll always call it "home." It's a special place sprung from your imagination and hard work. It is a refuge, sanctuary, memory vault and more. In the end, it's where you live your best barndominium life.

The Ultimate Barndominium Resource Guide

3D Global Design
3dglobaldesign.com
Building design services

Bunger Steel
www.bungersteel.com
(800) 328-6437
Manufacturer of premium steel buildings, including customized barndominiums

Back Forty Building Co.
backfortybuildings.com
Planning and design company that will design your barndominium and facilitate the manufacturing process

Carolina Post Frame Barndominiums
www.cpfbuildings.com
(803) 720-4385
Manufacturer of steel barndominiums and offers custom designs and consulting services

Cooperative Extension Service Offices
www.nifa.usda.gov/land-grant-colleges-and-universities-partner-website-directory
Government resource providing information on local topography and weather patterns

Cupolas Direct
cupolasdirect.com
(717) 808-5711
Supplier of wood, metal, and vinyl cupolas in a wide range of designs, including windows, louvers, and vents

FHA
fha.gov
Federal loan guarantee program to assist new home buyers in financing home purchases

General Steel Buildings
gensteel.com
(855) 426-9202
Manufacturer of metal building kits, including barndominiums in several different sizes and floor plans

Greiner Buildings
www.greinerbuildings.com
(888) 466-4139
Premium pole-barn building manufacturer, including barndominiums and standalone workshops

Heritage Building Systems
www.heritagebuildings.com
(800) 643-5555
Manufacturer of steel barndominium kits

JJ's Custom Builders
jjscustombuilders.com
(717) 740-9570
Pennsylvania-based builder well versed in converting existing barns to new living spaces, and building new barndominiums from the ground up

Kansas City Metal Buildings
kansascitymetalbuildings.com
(816) 597-4830
Texas-based builder of steel barndominiums

Lester Buildings

www.lesterbuildings.com

(800) 826-4439

Manufacturer of pole barns and post-frame prefab barndominium kits. Offers planning and financing guidance

Maverick Steel Buildings

mavericksteelbuildings.com

(706) 948-1924

Manufacturer of multiple sizes of barndominium kits

McElroy Metal

www.mcelroymetal.com

(318) 747-8000

Manufacturer of steel siding, roofing, and complete cold-formed bolt-up steel buildings

Our Barndominium Life

ourbarndominiumlife.com

(281) 592-0298

Barndominium design firm, offering custom design services, advice, and consultation on build issues

Panda Windows & Doors

www.panda-windows.com

(623) 267-9981

Manufacturer of doors and windows, including custom projects, with specific experience fabricating for barndominium use

Reaves Buildings

reavesbuildings.com

(800) 658-3572

Supplier of engineered wood-frame, prefab barndominium packages

R & R Iron Works

www.rrironworks.com

(828) 334-3507

Manufacturer of several barndominium kits in distinctly different styles

Salter Spiral Stair

www.salterspiralstair.com

(888) 416-1795

Manufacturer of spiral staircases with experience fabricating for barndominiums

SteelCo Buildings, Inc.

www.steelcobuildings.com

(866) 728-9973

Manufacturer of prefab steel buildings including bolt-up barndominium packages

SteelMaster Building Systems

www.steelmasterusa.com

(877) 342-1703

Manufacturer of unique Quonset-hut style barndominums

Summertown Metals

summertownmetals.com

(931) 796-1521

Supplier of barndominium components, plans, and packages

Texas Best Construction

www.texas-bestconstruction.com

(469) 552-8205

Premier custom barndominium builder provide turnkey services, including build-out and finishing

Timberlyne

www.timberlyne.com

(877) 680-1680

Custom timber-frame barndominiums, including entire shell components or just framing. Also provides on-site assistance.

USDA Rural Home Loan Program

www.rd.usda.gov/programs-services/single-family-housing-programs

United States Department of Agricultural program providing loans on attractive terms for rural, single-family homes

U.S. Geological Survey (USGS)

www.usgs.gov

(888) 392-8545

Part of the U.S. Department of the Interior, the USGS conducts monitoring and research into the country's topography. Government and individuals can use this information to make informed decisions about land management and other issues—such as whether to buy a particular plot of land.

USDA Rural Development / Electrical Programs

www.rd.usda.gov/programs-services/electric-programs

Grants, loans, and other programs to help with rural electrification

The Original Windmill Ceiling Fans

windmillceilingfans.com

(972) 834-5555

American-made, handcrafted windmill ceiling fans

VA

www.benefits.va.gov/homeloans/

US Department of Veteran Affairs offers a home loan program for individuals who have served in the military. Rates and terms may be better than those offered through traditional lenders.

Worldwide Steel Buildings

www.worldwidesteelbuildings.com

(800) 825-0316

A steel manufacturer, Worldwide fabricates its own steel building components. The company offers complete steel barndominium kits with customization options, shipped anywhere in the country.

Photo Credits

Photo courtesy of 3D Global Design & Back Forty Buildings, 3dglobaldesign.com/backfortybuildings.com

25 (top), 38–39, 86, 94–95, 163 (right)

Photo courtesy of Back Forty Building Co., backfortybuildings.com

21 (top), 23 (top), 28 (top), 29 (top), 32 (top), 33, 101 (bottom), 107, 185

Photo courtesy of Bunger Steel, www.bungersteel.com, (800) 328-6437

9, 13 (top), 22 (bottom), 30 (bottom), 62, 78, 105 (top and bottom right), 114, 183

Photo courtesy of Carolina Post Frame Barndominiums, www.cpfbuildings.com, (803) 720-4385

48, 124

Photo courtesy of Cupolas Direct, cupolasdirect.com, (717) 808-5711

99 (bottom), 126

Photo courtesy of Greiner Buildings, www.greinerbuildings.com, (888) 466-4139

6–7, 15 (top), 20, 23 (center), 44–45, 56–57, 88–89, 98, 182–183

Photo courtesy of Heritage Building Systems, www.heritagebuildings.com, (888) 905-6445

18–19, 34–35, 41, 60–61, 63, 90

Photo courtesy of Lester Building Systems LLC, www.lesterbuildings.com, (800) 826-4439

10, 26 (top left), 91, 122 (left)

About the Author

Chris Peterson is a veteran home improvement and design author. Among the many books he has written are *5-Gallon Bucket Book*, *Building with Secondhand Stuff*, *Manskills*, *Camper Rehab*, four books in the Ideas You Can Use series, and many books in Cool Springs Press's BLACK+DECKER Complete Guide series. He has also coauthored numerous home design books with noted media celebrities. He lives in Ashland, Oregon.

Index